Reflections of the
1960 to 1975
White Plains, NY

Memories of Two Who Know the Necessity of Friendship and Familyhood Whenever and Wherever We Are

Revised Edition

Joe L. Mack, B.A., M.A., USMC, USN (RET) MCPO(SW)

and

Jamal R. Koram, B.A., M.S., Ed.S.

WINBROOK PRIDE

By Jamal Koram, (Baba Jamal) Ed.S.

Just a patch of Knowing that

It took longer to create our beloved homes of brick

Than to build a protective neighborhood

Where memories stick

Find a story and pass it on for you know who we are

Those who are coming, and those who are gone

Find the land and neighborhood

Recall the past, be it understood

That Winbrook is more than brick

It's family ties

It's "Still I Rise"

It's Spirit and Prayer

Deposited everywhere HERE and THERE

And north and south and east and west…and may those who have passed have

eternal rest

TABLE OF CONTENTS

DEDICATIONS

Baba Jamal's Dedication

Dedicated to Mama Mary Mack and Mama Marjoric Rogers, Maude Miller/Carrie Hankinson/Muriel, Tommy and Ethel Carter, Ethel and Earl Cole, Sr., Mrs. Foster, and Willie Foster and siblings, Dr. Grandmaster Shihan Willie Mack, L. Carolyn Moore, and family, and all of us who made it through, even if only for a little while.

Bless the Coram family on Warren Avenue, Greenburgh, and in other towns, villages, cities, and states.

Special thanks to our immediate families, who supported our visions, our research trips, and our dedication to the "Winbrook Years," in the city of White Plains. Also extending thanks to our relatives, Grandparents, and Grand Aunts and Uncles, and cousins, and friends in surrounding cities and towns in Westchester County, New York.

DEDICATED to those who left this journey sooner than expected …and to those who held on long enough for us to wipe our tears and remember the times of strength and creativity. For those of us who needed to explore other environs in other times; and for those who we can walk up to in front of one of the five buildings, or during Juneteenth, folks and buildings that are left. Or maybe, get in touch and keep in touch wherever we are, and to remember the good and the bad times, and to greet those who live where they grew into adulthood, and seniority …And maybe to go to a church service at one of the old churches that are still standing strong, or maybe one of the new ones that grew up in the neighborhood, or maybe someone that is waiting for one of us to visit, and not to just talk about the old times, but to remember, shed some tears, and enjoy some laughter…Or maybe go to someplace that is still there…Maybe Star Diner, that, after the prom in 1968, when Trina, Carolyn, Glen, and James went there for an after-prom breakfast, and one of the old champion boxers, Cleo Daniels, paid for our early morning meals as the music box played:

"Spinning Around (I Must Be Falling in Love)" by The Main Ingredient.

Love and Blessings to those who are here, and for those who have come and gone, who have never left our hearts, nor our memories…

Our love and respect for the Foster Family, those here and those gone…

TO WILLIE FOSTER AND HIS MOTHER…MAY THEY REST IN PEACE. Bless his siblings and family.

Had he been here, this project would have more names, events, and historical accuracy because Willie had that kind of genius. In addition, he was a mathematical expert on all levels, and in almost every aspect of mathematics. His recall and intelligence were phenomenal.

A few weeks earlier, I was in White Plains, working on this project when Willie took me to see his mother. Which was shortly before her departure. Mama Foster was in a different apartment but the same building at 135 South Lexington Avenue. She was glad to see me and vice versa. During my stay, I told them of the project Joe Mack, and I were working on and said we should interview them as well.

A list that my "close one," Brother Willie Foster left, when we first started the idea of a memory book…or was it someone else? No, it was Willie. I know for sure that he had another list that he was writing when I first brought the idea to him. Willie and I started talking about the book project and he began writing names on an index card …we stayed for a while.

In the short time we talked about this project, Willie listed over sixty names of folks. We were supposed to meet, later that year…It was the last time I saw either one of them… and at seventy years old… I still weep.

God Bless the Family, and other families and friends, who made our lives bearable and enjoyable, and memorable… Amen.

Joe Mack's Dedications:

To my mother, Ms. Mary Mack, building 159, who brought me into this world, raised us in a single-parent household, and to whom I owe everything I have become. She was one of those strong Black women you only read about who refused to let the challenges of today's society keep her from raising her family with respect, dignity, grounded in their spiritual foundation, and with a strong sense of determination.

My father, Willie Mack, Sr. who was in our life for a time as well and taught us some valuable lessons.

My brother, Grandmaster Shihan Dr. W. Mack, who was always there whenever I needed him and who rose from his young days of training to become one of the greatest Karate Masters of all time. His philosophy, wisdom, and concern for his community make him a rare exception and an inspiration to many. He taught me to be strong in the face of adversity, and he always believed in me.

My sister, Lillie Holiday, who lives in Connecticut and someone I was close to all my life. We grew up making sure we looked out for each other and she is someone who always knew how to make me laugh.

My wonderful wife, Thelma, and our children, Gamal, Imani, and Tahir. Thank you all for being there for me throughout the course of this book as you have always been. You are the reason I find the strength to go on every day and without your encouragement, motivation, and love I would be lost.

Special dedication to our ancestors and loved ones who are no longer with us but whose spirits still live on within us and provide inspiration and encouragement each day.

ACKNOWLEDGEMENTS

Special thanks to Thelma A. Mack, my wife, who devoted her time and energy to help the authors with formatting, review editing, and transcribing interviews over many hours to ensure the successful completion of this book. Her expertise and literary experience made our journey so much better as she helped guide us along the way.

Special thanks to Natasha Underdue who developed the artistic rendition of the cover for *Reflections of the Winbrook Years* and dedicated herself to meticulous completion of the same. As an accomplished and talented artist, Natasha met with the authors and used her creativity to design a book cover that captured the essence of the five buildings described in the story.

Special thanks to our families, relatives, and friends who have always encouraged us to be the best we can be.

Families who have touched my life in a special way:
- The Mitchell Family, Bldg. 135 South Lexington Ave and Lake St. Apts.
- The Twine Family, Greenwich, CT
- The Williams Family, Bldg. 33 Fisher Ave.
- The Livingston Family, Bldg. 159 South Lexington Ave.
- The Mack Family, Bldg. 159 South Lexington Ave., 4th floor
- The Sudderth Family, Greenburgh, NY
- The Archer Family, Greenburgh, NY
- The James Family, Greenburgh, NY
- The Rooke Family, Bldg. 159 South Lexington Ave.
- The Higgs Family, Bldg. 159 South Lexington Ave.
- The Hodge Family, Sumter, SC
- The Holiday Family, Sumter, SC
- The Rush Family, Sumter, SC
- Rev. Phifer and Family, Calvary Baptist
- Rev. Cousins and Family, Calvary Baptist

- Rev. Smalls and Family, Calvary Baptist

Special Acknowledgement and A Note of Gratitude:

We want to extend a special thanks to all the folks we met with, talked to, interviewed, or otherwise provided some helpful information to make this book possible. Your time, efforts, and thoughts are greatly appreciated and played a significant role in helping us capture true *Reflections of the Winbrook Years* in their purest form. Listed below are some of the people we can recall. Please forgive any omissions knowing it to be only an error of the head and not the heart.

- Ben Himmelfarb, Librarian I, White Plains Library.

Ben arranged our original interview space at the library in the early stages of this project. He was instrumental in providing us with a wealth of historical documents of which the most prominent was "Racial Confrontation", a study of the 1968 White Plains, New York, High School Student Boycott, in which many of us participated.

- Kathy Degyansky, Assistant Library Director, White Plains Library.

Kathy arranged for our final interviews in White Plains to be conducted in the library and provided invaluable assistance with planning for future programs and book signings when the project is completed.

The three people below arranged for us to hold several workshops and meetings at the Thomas H. Slater Community Center while providing us with a home base from which to operate during our many visits to White Plains while collecting information for this project. Without their support, we surely would have faced a much greater challenge obtaining the content information needed for this book.

- Heather Miller, Director, Thomas H. Slater Community Center, Inc. White Plains, New York

- Hurvy E. Bradshaw, Assistant Director, Thomas H. Slater Community Center, White Plains, New York

- Anita Roper, Administrative Assistant, Thomas H. Slater Community Center, White Plains, New York

Others who provided notable input to the project include, but are not limited to:

- Valerie Simmons, WPHS class of 70
- Cliff Livingston, WPHS class of 69
- Brother Suryaj Peterson, White Plains Community Organizer
- Artie Bennett, WPHS class of 68
- Wilbur Rooke, WPHS class of 70
- Gamal Mack, WPHS class of 88
- Jason Rhodes, WPHS class of 88
- Rick Roberts, Woodlands HS class of 1971
- Billy Sudderth III, Woodlands HS class of 68
- Alden Mitchell, Woodlands HS class of 68
- Charlie Morgan, WPHS class of 69
- Warren Harry, WPHS class of 69
- Master Bahru Seward, Universal Goju Ryu Kai School
- Grandmaster Shihan Dr. W. Mack, Head of Universal Goju Ryu Kai School
- Grandmaster Tony Watts, Wing Chun School of Self Defense

FORWARD

In the harshest sense, America has been lived and experienced differently by its citizens, largely based on Race. Fredrick Douglass once asked the question; "What is the Fourth of July to a Slave?" The inherent answer recognizes the realities of two Americas; one free, the other oppressed. What must it be to be a part of that underclass, then and now; formerly enslaved, formerly freed, formerly glorious, segregated, marginalized?

The premise could easily be mistaken as natural and organic. But there is a time before America, other lands, Kingdoms, cultures, civilizations. Ancient Greece had slaves along ethnic, not racial lines. Ideas of worthy and unworthy cropped as an attempted justification, Aristotle believed in the Supremacy of Greece and that everyone else, other than Greek Citizens, were Barbarians. This was contrary to Herodotus' account when referring to Ethiopia; "this country produces great quantities of gold, has an abundance of elephants and all the woodland trees, and ebony; and its men are the tallest, the most handsome, and the longest-lived." (Despite the accounts of beautiful people, glorious Nubians by his counterparts.) This current America that I refer to, stretches back to the 1600s. The notion of race, the emergence of White Supremacist ideas took root in the Spanish Inquisition, five hundred years ago, policies, practices, pseudo-science employed for the purpose of pursuing and gaining riches.

The truth was buried, hidden; kingdoms of Kush, Mali, Songhai, Egypt, for example, were hidden; its learning centers like Timbuktu.

There have been generations of people with varied lives in varied places, one of those places is White Plains, New York. Pinpointing any specific time or place may require a magnifying glass, a singular focus of the time, its influences, music, rhythm, economic stratification, policies, etc., the people, and how they specifically experienced life.

How people lived, celebrated, coped, intermingled, loved, worshipped, shared time and space is what is important in life.

The use of Race from the 15th Century forward has been used to bind, limit, define, and negatively shape the World and its inhabitants

White Plains played its role in history, the creation/establishment of New York State, the Battle of White Plains/George Washington, somewhat of a respite in the Great Migration (1916-1970). Many Blacks from the South made their way North, hoping to escape the open terror and other horrid expressions of the South; lynchings, suppression, disparate treatment by every deputized white person who felt it their right to subjugate.

What of the people, who Curtis Mayfield referred to as "We the People Who Are Darker than Blue," a people who lived, sung, created the "Blues," later Rock and Roll, and Rap/Hip Hop from their experience. An outward expression of their joy, pain, and angst.

How did they live, what did they love, what was their experience? These are the questions this book seeks to answer. Now, of course, every story can't be told, every person remembered, but it is the hope to remember, celebrate, honor, and reflect on a specific place, a specific time, by sharing the remembrance.

Traditionally, history has been skewed and told only by the victor about the King or Queen or some symbol of that in the most biased light, often conferring some divine status that absolves human foibles.

White Plains began as a Village, later incorporated as a City. An important historical place where George Washington held ground and made the British retreat. Previously purchased from Native Americans. Immigration in the 1910s. The building of I-287, the Bronx River Parkway, Railroad Stations, and Gedney Resort made White Plains an ideal town with access to New York City. Its population exploded in the 1920s, stagnated in the 1930s Great Depression, rallied in the 1940s due to WW II, Urban Renewal in the 1950s, the destruction of Brookfield Street, Black homes, Black businesses, mom and pop stores, and a new uniform vision of commerce. Winbrook was built in the 1950s, a racial reckoning in the 1960s, the Vietnam War, the building of the Summit House/Ferris, and Lake Street. A City largely becoming affluent. Parades sponsored by large anchor stores like Macy's, Movie Houses along the way all sorts of societal organizations, Veterans groups, Centers, social service programs, the second High School (195) being built on North Street, replacing Highlands.

But what of the people

Particularly the people who are "Darker than Blue"

This is their story, in a particular time, place, and experience.

By: Jason Rhodes, Attorney at Law, White Plains High School, Class of 1988

INTRODUCTION

By Joe Mack

Practically all cities in the United States have housing developments designed to house large numbers of people within a collective community. These developments vary in size and scope from city to city depending on the needs of city planning for the development and the space available to build them.

They do, however, have several things in common. They are often located at or near the downtown vicinity. They generally will provide housing for various income levels ranging from those who can afford to pay a higher rent to those who cannot and may need to have their rent subsidized by state or federal programs. So yes, it's true that all families living in these housing developments do not pay the same amount for rent.

The other thing they have in common is that the larger percentage of families in these developments will generally be minorities, with the rest coming from various cultures and backgrounds.

These developments are generally managed by a housing authority in the city and have commonly become known as "The Projects," in most communities over the years. It's also important to note that all projects are not the same. A housing development in Detroit may be vastly different from one in Philadelphia or New York or Mississippi in terms of size, living conditions, cost, and environment.

While this manuscript will provide some insight about one housing development in New York, "The Winbrook Apartments in White Plains, NY" managed by the White Plains Housing Authority, it could just as easily be applied to life in any other city in the U.S.

Winbrook was home to the authors of this book, Baba Jamal Koram "The

StoryMan" and Joe "Lukata" Mack, who hope to directly touch on the lives of the people they knew growing up in White Plains and indirectly provide a moment of reflection for others who can see themselves and the lives of their own community through the similarities found within.

The writers hope to accomplish this by reaching out and touching the very soul of the City of White Plains, NY, commonly known as "Winbrook" and compassionately referred to as "The Projects" located in White Plains, NY, the center of the County Seat of Westchester, NY. Enjoy the journey as you travel with them through the life, times, and experiences of two young Black males, during roughly the years of 1960 through 1975, who grew up in White Plains around that time.

Throughout the course of this book, you will find the authors referred to in several different ways.

Joe L. Mack will generally be listed as Joe, Joe Lewis, Joe Mack, or occasionally "Lukata".

Jamal R. Koram will be referred to as Baba Jamal, Jamal Koram, Jamal, or James Coram from time to time, with an occasional reference to "Looney".

Interviews:

In addition to numerous meetings and discussions, several key interviews were conducted during the process of this work and will be represented by excerpts throughout the book or included by summary as a complete section.

Interviews were recorded with:

1. Richard (Rick) A. Roberts, MBA, JD. Nick is now a financial consultant in White Plains who grew up and attended school at Woodlands High in Greenburg, NY. Rick's input sheds significant light on events in the community and especially on the role of his father, Doyle Roberts, who was a mainstay in the business community of his day.

2. Valerie Simmons. Valerie is a graduate of White Plains High who spent her entire youth in Winbrook and who grew up to become the property manager of the White Plains Housing Authority for the Winbrook complex. Valerie provided invaluable insight to this project which could only be found in someone of her experience and

level of expertise.

3. Gamal (Doc) Mack. Gamal was also a graduate of White Plains High and someone who spent his entire youth in Winbrook. Gamal's contribution will be an enlightening reflection into the days of his era, class of 1988 while providing an interesting look at the transition of life in Winbrook and around White Plains from the '70s and into the '80s and beyond.

4. Jason Rhodes. Jason grew up in Winbrook as a child and is also a product of White Plains High School. He is now an attorney who lives in Maryland and is an accomplished author in his own right. Growing up in Winbrook, 135 So. Lexington Ave, like Gamal, he lived through the life experiences of the '70s, '80s, and years thereafter. We found Jason uniquely qualified by his life experiences and were honored to have him provide the forward for this book. Additionally, Jason contributed an astounding rendition of Martial Arts entitled "Return to the 36 Chamber...For Real" which will be found in its entirety during the reading of these chapters.

5. Larry Albert. A young man from Mamaroneck, NY who spent much of his time in White Plains and who knew several friends from the projects and surrounding areas. Larry was a standout in Track and Field at Rye Neck High School in Mamaroneck and therefore knew, or knew of, nearly all the track stars from White Plains High. Larry was also a member of several bands as a singer and performed alongside bands from White Plains like the Societies and the Sensations during the Show Mobiles in the summers.

CHAPTER 1

HOW THE JOURNEY BEGAN: PURPOSE AND EXPECTATIONS

Joe Mack's Beginning Journey & Names of People He Knew

Memoirs of My Winbrook Experience

by Joe Mack

Today I am a retired Navy Master Chief and Marine Corps veteran who lives in Virginia. When people ask me where I'm from, I often tell them I was born and raised in South Carolina in a small town called Sumter, but I grew up through my teenage years and became a man when I moved with my mother, Ms. Mary Mack, to White Plains, NY.

The following is a collection of my memories and reflections of that transition as part of a collaborative work being done in conjunction with my co-author and close friend, Baba Jamal Koram, 'The StoryMan,'' who is also from the White Plains region and a person who has been an inspiration and instrumental in my life in many ways.

This documentary will focus on roughly the years 1960 – 1975 and will reflect, to some degree, day to day life of a young Black man growing up in White Plains but will mainly focus on the life and times of those who lived in the five buildings of the Winbrook Housing Authority, commonly referred to as "The Projects."

Those five buildings became the heart and soul of Black folks in and around White Plains. Just about every family in the area either lived in the projects or knew somebody who did. There were friends, family members, cousins, brothers, sisters, uncles, aunts, and so on, with connections, in some way, to the projects. These connections extended throughout the entire community of Westchester County to include areas like Greenburgh, Yonkers, Dobbs Ferry, Port Chester, Mount Vernon, Ossining, Tarrytown, Mamaroneck, New Rochelle, and yes, even Scarsdale (a high-income, high profile and predominately White neighborhood).

The five buildings were known by their street addresses, such as 159 South Lexington Avenue, 11 Fisher Avenue, 135 South Lexington Avenue, 33 Fisher Avenue, 225 Grove Street, and each of them will be expounded on further as we go deeper into the "Winbrook Experience".

I can reflect on my journey which began around the age of 13 starting with my first residence in White Plains being on Ridge Street, which was at the very end of Lexington Avenue. I later learned that White Plains was sort of broken down into several communities, as far as Black folks were concerned, and Ridge Street was located close to the Ferris Avenue community.

This meant I first got to know the people who lived in that area of White Plains. Folks like Billy Walker, Irving, and Jerome "Bump" Robinson, Wayne, Reggie, and a host of others. Billy Walker's house was the most centrally located so in the afternoons and on weekends we would all meet on his porch and make our plans for the day.

This often included playing a game called "Around the World, Bunkie's Up" on the Lexington Avenue basketball court. If you were the last to make all your baskets from the designated spots on the court, you had to stand by the equipment shed with your head on the wall, and your rear end sticking up, while the other players got to throw the ball as hard as they could at your well-defined target! Since my basketball strength was defense and the finger roll (I hadn't fully developed a reliable jump shot) I got to spend more than my fair share of time on "the wall".

My next official residence in White Plains would be on Spring Street but I also experienced a significant social development period during this time, and that's when the "growing up" began. This was when I got my first formal introduction to the Winbrook Projects. Oh yes, I had heard about them and knew where they were, but I had no burning desire to go in that direction. You had to be from there or know someone who was, and if you didn't know anyone, there was a good chance you wouldn't make it past one of the buildings without ending up in a confrontation with someone. I remember the first time I walked past 135 and 159 Lexington Avenue, I walked on the other side of the street just to check it out.

Now, I was a pretty "tough brother" myself who didn't have a lot of fear, but the looks I got told me it wouldn't be in my best interest to go across the street and try to walk through the crowd at that time.

My foray into the projects came because my mother, who worked as a home care nurse, was assigned to take care of an elderly lady named Ms. Rowels, who lived alone at 33 Fisher Avenue. She lived on the 9th floor of that building in apartment 9-H, I believe, which soon became my hangout and where I began to make friends.

My younger sister, Lillie was also there and as a result, I got to know the girls who were her friends. Among the first girls I met in the building were Amanda Pearl Williams and Carolyn Ravenelle; both became close friends, and I ultimately became known as their big brother as well and Godfather to Pearl's only son "Toby." When I think of the elders who kept an eye on us and who taught us to respect ourselves and others within the Winbrook community, Pearl's mother, Ms. Williams, is one of the first to come to mind.

I met most of the guys I encountered and later befriended at the projects downstairs on the playground where the basketball courts were located. This was the central meeting place throughout the day and on weekends and was relatively calm most of the time until the games began. This became the training grounds for the New York Poles and later the JABO RIMS, our Winbrook basketball teams which dominated the region for a season or so…more on that to follow.

I mentioned Spring Street, which is where we lived while waiting for a place to become available in the projects. Our name was on the waiting list, but it took time, so much time in fact, I had finished high school, gone to war in Viet Nam, and returned before a spot became available.

Spring Street is now converted into stores and a shopping complex called the White Plains Mall, but I have lasting memories of that location as well. Before Spring Street, we lived in a two-family house on Cambridge Avenue, off Lexington Avenue, which is where I was staying when I graduated from high school.

So you can see that my family, like many others, moved around in White Plains a lot, out of necessity more so than desire, before finally settling in at Winbrook, 159 South Lexington Avenue, apartment 8G. This would become our home for many years thereafter. It was not uncommon for Black families in the area to move a lot during that time. We now know that our parents were doing all they could in a difficult environment to make ends meet and to give their children the best chance they could to succeed in life.

This constant family movement was largely due to what they called the "Urban Renewal Project," meaning that if the city planners saw an area in the city they wanted to develop, they simply notified the families living in that area how long they had before those houses would be taken over by urban renewal. The families would then usually have around six to nine months or so to find somewhere else to live. I'm sure it was a little more complicated than that, but to me as a young child, that's how I saw it. You lived in a house or an apartment, and your parents would get a notice that urban renewal was planning to develop that area and would give them a deadline in which they had to move. As a result of these changes, streets like Winchester Avenue, Spring Street, Ridge Street, Cambridge Avenue, and Brookfield Street are all now gone, with many families, like us, moving into Winbrook from those areas.

Somehow Ferris Avenue was spared of this fate and remained pretty much intact.

Now, of course, this didn't affect people who owned their homes to my knowledge, and then again, their neighborhoods weren't being redeveloped like the other areas around White Plains that were considered ideal locations to build malls, police stations, shopping centers, and the like. This is how the Galleria Mall, the current police station, White Plains Mall, White Plains Library, and yes, even the Westchester County Courthouse all came to be…Brookfield St. is no more!

The Winbrook Projects no longer exist as we once knew them. Baba Jamal and I recently watched 135 South Lexington Avenue fall to the ground… Still, the memories of the days we lived there, the folks we knew who taught us how to survive there, and the sense of community we developed among each other will last forever and will always be cherished.

This brings to mind a phrase once quoted by The Reverend Al Sharpton on his XM radio station. He said, "The best way to find yourself is to lose yourself in something BIGGER than yourself." This message speaks volumes when it comes to our thoughts on preserving the legacy of Winbrook.

This book is a collaboration by Baba Jamal Koram (The StoryMan) a.k.a. "Looney" (not related to the "Looney" family in the Valley) and, Joe Mack, with an aim to do just that; preserve the Legacy of those that came before us, and those that came with us, who laid the foundations for us to build on. We hope to capture these memories so that they don't go the way of the buildings, several of which have been torn down or converted into high-rise condos, affordable only to those who are well off enough to financially obtain them.

As we begin to see the buildings laid to rest or converted into condos, we'll try to reflect on the way things used to be. The five buildings were laid out in such a manner that they formed a circle leading to the playground… this "circle" also reflected how close the families were who lived in Winbrook.

Yes, we had our squabbles on the playground, from time to time, but if you lived in any of the five buildings, you were part of a network that encompassed ALL the buildings. Everyone looked out for each other; the elders corrected any of the children when needed and nobody talked back or disrespected them. That was life in the Winbrook Projects, we understood that the term "let the circle be unbroken" applied to us all.

I recall during one of our recent visits to White Plains to meet with folks and conduct interviews, Baba Jamal and I walked around our old neighborhood to see how things had changed and he commented, "Not only has the circle been broken, the circle is gone." That thought stuck with me and our prayer is that, through these memoirs and the recollections by others like them, unlike the circle, memories of the Winbrook experience will never be "gone."

Reflections of How Joe Mack and James Coram Met

By Baba Jamal

Our Roots: South Carolina …

Joe and Jamal connected in their senior year at WPHS, especially because it was discovered that both of their mothers were from South Carolina, about forty miles from each other. Joe was born and lived his early years in South Carolina before coming to White Plains, NY. Mama Mack, Joe, and Jamal took a trek to South Carolina one year… what a time we had! Pressing on the brakes in the car only to find there was "nothing there" and having to tell Mama Mack they wouldn't be able to stop! Man, that didn't go over too well!

Brother Koram and Joe Mack have made several round trips from White Plains to their ancestral homes on their mothers' side of the family. Both of their mothers were born and raised in South Carolina, not far from each other. Another coincidence was that at one point before moving to Winbrook, the Macks lived on Spring Street, little after the time Baba Jamal's Aunt Lessie from South Carolina lived on the corner of Spring Street!

Joe and Jamal's connection grew, more so, after high school than during high school. The friendship expanded when Jamal's counselor, Mr. Pollock, and his wife, took them to an educational organization near Delancey Street in NY City. The organization's main focus was to prepare students for college admission and to get them into colleges anywhere in the country.

The more they connected the greater their friendship grew. At one point, they drove from South Carolina and back to Winbrook, Ferris Avenue, the Valley, and Greenburgh. That trip solidified their friendship even more. OH! And on one trip to White Plains, they picked up a mutual friend, "Billy" Sudderth III. Billy and Joe, both went to boot camp in Parris Island and at Camp Lejeune in the Marine Corps during the same time. Billy and Baba Jamal's cousins, Carol Coram, and her family lived next door to one another…a small world indeed.

Joe Mack's Methodology:

This will be a compilation of stories, reflections, and interviews collected over approximately the past five years or so which encompassed several trips to White Plains for that purpose. In addition, we have also communicated with several White Plains residents who have since relocated to other states such as North Carolina, Virginia, Georgia, Florida, and Maryland. These residents made valuable contributions to the project as well. You will also find the summation of several live recorded interviews dispersed throughout the book which serves to enhance the content and provide a personal perspective of life in and around the five buildings during that time. Finally, we were able to communicate with generations both before and after our time to obtain their input, which helped us to bridge the generational gap as a matter of adding bookends to the experiences during our time in Winbrook.

Throughout this book, we will explore several aspects of community life in and around the Winbrook community. These will include a random selection of thoughts on the following matters in no particular order:

Reflections of Life in and around The Projects

The influence of Churches, Spiritual or Religious Growth

Respect for Others and Our Elders

Schools, Education, and Programs in the Community

How We Socialized with Others in the Community and the City of White Plains

Dangerous Times and Drugs

Law Enforcement and Tragedy

The Impact of Sports in School and on the Professional Level

Racial Unrest of 1968 - 70 in the City and at the High Schools

Protest and Leaders of the Movement in the City: The Days of JABO

Greenburg and White Plains; Joint Experiences and Relationships

The Introduction of Martial Arts and Self Defense Schools to the Community

Summer Activities and Caddying at the Golf Course

White Plains High, Woodlands, and some of the College Experiences that Followed

Military Experiences

Meeting at the Recreation Centers for Fun on the Weekends

The Cage Recreation and Boxing Gym

The Night Clubs and Other Entertainment

The following topics will also be given their just due; Saxon Woods, Rye Playland, Trips to the City, The Loews and RKO movie theaters, The Mamaroneck Ave Pizza Shoppe, The White Plains Taxi and Red Top Taxi companies, Joint Action for Black Organization (JABO), Community Action Program (CAP) with a special section dedicated to the "Brothers and Sisters Who Passed This Way" and are no longer with us, except in spirit and truth. While this list is in no way complete or would claim to have captured everyone who affected or had an impact on our community, we hope to have captured a reasonable sampling of those who did. Any omissions are in no way intentional and only serve as a function of the loss of memory or contact due to the years that have gone by.

Baba Jamal's Methodology

At the beginning of our research, we were just going to list names of male and female friends, and maybe cite an event or two. It was eventually realized that, in doing so, we wouldn't have a memoir, just a list of names. So, here we are. We trust that you too, will have some joyful recall, along with the tears of remembrance, and sadness, that will in some way, bring what in recent years, has been called "Winbrook Pride." Hopefully, in the tears we shed, remembering, AND in recalling joyful and sad times, and in "Walking Winbrook," with smiles we had in being thankful for knowing the personalities, here and gone. Now, we will include some of the sisters, quite frankly, most of the males hung out daily with each other, knuckleheads, cool breezes, etc. Those that had enlisted in the military or who were jailed, when another group stepped up. We also had a Sisterhood, the "The Dirty Dozen," that was no joke!

Some of the information, feedback, and memories came from folks who lived outside of Winbrook on adjoining side streets - Brookfield, Winchester, Lexington Avenue, Fisher Avenue, Spring St., Post Road, etc. Relatives, from near and far. Folks from the other surrounding neighborhoods such as Ferris Ave, the Valley, Battle Hill, and other communities, and townships, all had a connection of some sort within the Winbrook environment in White Plains, New York, which is the County Seat of Westchester County, in the state of New York.

Joe Mack's mother and my mother were both born in South Carolina. Both came to White Plains, with family and a dream.

My mother was living primarily in Greenburgh, Brooklyn, and NYC. My mother's sister, our Aunt Lessie, from Holly Hill, South Carolina, was living on Spring Street in White Plains. Other cousins lived in Winbrook building 225.

There were two "Mack" families that we know of in Winbrook. They were not related…but to make things more complicated, they both lived in 159 and both families had boxing and martial arts backgrounds. Kenny, Freddy and, them were boxers. Both trained at the "Cage." The Cage was a boxing and martial arts gym in White Plains, off Main Street. Joe Mack trained and boxed there as well.

Sensei William Mack, Joe's brother, was, and is, a world-renowned Karate Shihan. He is noted to have been awarded several Belts and titles, including Grandmaster and the highest awards for his skills and /or for his accomplishments and achievements, ultimately inducted into the Oriental World of Self Defense Martial Arts Hall of Fame by Great Grandmaster Arron Banks at Madison Square Garden in New York. And to top it off, Joe Mack was a competitive boxer, who is also highly skilled in the martial arts.

CHAPTER 2

REFLECTIONS: MEMORIES OF PEOPLE, PLACES, AND EVENTS

Schools, Social spots, Recreation entries, Nightclubs, and other entertainment

Preserving a Legacy of Encouragement

Baba Jamal:

Joe Mack and I both wanted to give honor and grace, to this certain time period, called the sixties, and to the many people who affected our lives. Folks we shared joy, sadness, happiness, and PRIDE with…For those that made it to age 30 plus…and for those who didn't, but whose memories, along with our gratefulness, bring us peace.

Remembering the people, and the time. Not to shed tears but to remember… and shed some tears. "It's ok…"

This is the beginning of the Winbrook Years. A collection of memories of places, people, activities, events, and occurrences as seen through our memories. The emotions are real. In some cases, the names of individuals, groups, or families were either left out or abbreviated. The memories are ours. The events may be muted. The names of individuals or families were chosen so as not to embarrass, or to relive sorrowful, or painful events or activities but to reflect on and honor those we knew. In some cases, we have selected memories …some that could be remembered. For example, many may not remember "Buckets" Leroy, but if you know the projects, you can visualize him throwing a football from the ground onto the roof of "135". And it was accurate! We have chosen the time spans that we have clear memories of. The period we have chosen; however, we realize is almost too late to remember. Forgive us, if you will, for these are your memories as well as ours.

Remembering is caring. We care; therefore, we carry memories. We carry memories and we celebrate events and happenings that we recall…that we remember. We recall personalities and loved ones. The five buildings called Winbrook, the county seat of Westchester County, White Plains, New York, represent for us, not only a space within the buildings and of the people, but it also represents a special time that created personalities of education, music, sports, politics, the military, and racial pride. These ideas didn't just happen yesterday, they were discovered, embraced, and passed on.

Even as we read this, there are stories and memories that can be told by 50 years of generations that entered "the village," and never forgot Winbrook Pride!

Joe Mack and Jamal Koram have been friends since the days when Jamal was called Looney, (no relation to the family named Looney who lived in the "Valley"). Otis Moore, who lived in building 159 called him Looney because he walked with a crooked leg and a limp. Otis was young and he and his friends loved to be chased, figure that one out. Anyway, that nickname stuck, "Looney." To this day, Baba Jamal is known as Looney.

Joe Mack's family was highly respected. Some would say it was because his brother was Sensei Mack, a world-renown karate expert. Of course, there was respect for that fact, but Joe Mack was a personality himself and was a respected Boxer phenom at the "Cage." If that wasn't enough his mother, Mama Mary Mack was much respected for doing community work with the cub scouts and the Red Cross, her church activities, and being a good neighbor.

Baba Jamal's Winbrook Reflections:

Baba Jamal:

Forty-two years is a long time to carry a memory, but not as long as forever.

We have a clear understanding, knowing that we have influenced all neighborhoods in White Plains, New York, Westchester County, and the surrounding cities. The Winbrook Complex was the center of our universe, and the architect of our memories that will outlive the demolition of five buildings but not of the people who lived there, and for those who were there every day, and who lived in the surrounding areas in the hills of White Plains. Let it be known that building 135 left the Winbrook universe this past summer, 2020.

May our memories of happiness and sadness re-surface of you, the two of us, and our many friends. May our challenges and changes flitter in gladness only to shiver in sadness for a little while, our weeping is not that of a child…it is knowing, and releasing, and remembering just for a while, for we are grown now…so we sniff, and tears trickle only for a little while, and the deep breath we take, makes us feel BLESSED and good like we knew that it would. Peace be still now… Mama Foster/ Willie and Mama Mack and Mama Cole and Mama Maude Miller and Mama Rhodes and Mama Moore (north and south) and Mama Rogers and Mama Myers and Mama Maude and Kentucky Mama Miller and Mama Carter and Mama Gertrude and Aunt Alice and all Mamas who loved me/smothered me for just a little while, even Mama Ellease. Amen.

Blessings to all of y'all.

May our families, and our friends reunite in spirit and where and when we can gather, if only for a little while. Can you dig it? AMEN!

My reputation exceeded activities, so I let them fly. Even though the activities were bad enough. I found out who my real father was, but I couldn't tell anybody, so I let it fly. It was too late anyway, I was intelligent, rebellious, street affected, and had a quick mind, and a fast mouth. Some of it I used to get next to certain folks, and some of it I used as an extension from my early days in the New York City, Chelsea district in Brooklyn, and Harlem…Then one day in NYC on West 28th Street, where six of us lived in a one-room/small kitchen "not an apartment" my life changed.

I found a ten-dollar bill on the sidewalk, which took my sister Joyce and me from NYC to the Westchester County Office Building, to a foster home in Greenburgh on Washington Avenue. We never saw our mother again. I've been "Mothered" by many since then, have always pondered my life with the "Real Thing" of motherhood.

So, I came from NY City, REMEMBERED and learned the country ways of Greenburgh, (fruit trees, back yards, pet dog and cat, dirt roads) living with Mable and my sister Joyce, where I shared a bedroom with Eugene and Lorenzo, and Prince the cat, dropping gifts of mice on my bed. Me planting gardens…we never saw our mother again. We heard about her from a family friend, who years later drove us to my mother's funeral …but we got there too late.

But before that, after Greenburgh, the NEXT STEP! White Plains, NY! Orchard Parkway, Wyanoke Street, and five high-rise buildings, called Winbrook. What a journey. A hoodlum growing in the process of moving here and there, thank God Mrs. Elaine knew my Grandmother who barely knew me, I found the Coles in 135 just in time before I turned into a full-time hoodlum, and became a singer instead, with Darryl, not remembering playing with him on Brookfield and Martine until I saw a photo there. Later, we sang and danced on Show Mobiles …We almost made it to California …

WHERE DO WE START?

The Projects, as a whole, was a five-building homestead, a monument in the 1960s. Each building was identified by its address, i.e., 135, 159, 33, 11, and 225. And during this time, there was so much activity in downtown White Plains, and new shopping areas, new buildings, the old courthouse building was demolished, and so were other buildings and landscapes in "Old White Plains" … The lack of care for the Projects, it was just a matter of time for Winbrook, so they thought. What to do with the Negroes? They didn't know where to put us. With new construction downtown, a new courthouse location, new architecture, downtown, and construction for the new High School, which, subsequently, changed the old High School into the new Middle School. The old high school building was so large, and built in such a rectangular way, that the middle school track team could practice running long distances indoors around the upstairs hallways. Do we flush them out? That is, let the buildings just demolish. That didn't work, and a new government came in and suggestions were made to reestablish Winbrook. It almost worked, but where will the Negroes WORK? If anywhere at all? How do we transport them to the High School, Middle School, AND to the elementary school, etc., etc., etc?

Baba Jamal, in the past, was known by many nicknames, Looney, James, Jimmy, Crip, or Sonny, and the Prophet. And I'm sure there were a few other names that we'll leave alone. Relatives called him "Sonny" …not to be confused with "Big Sonny," the bus driver, who lived in the Valley a few doors away from the Moores'. Aunt Alice and them, who were family. My Uncle Harry married one of her daughters. Years later, and up in age, Aunt Alice moved into 33 Fisher, in Winbrook Housing. She always walked upright with a cane. She was given much respect, as were all of the elders that I am aware of during that time.

But where do we start remembering? Recalling the people, places, activities, the ups and downs, the good times and bad times. Both Brother Joe Mack and I decided to capture the Winbrook memories that we were and continue to be, part of. Those years, in the sixties, were memorable for several reasons. They were years of change and growth and they were times that right after our high school graduation we saw friends go to war. Some were not returning. Others returned with scars, while some returned as heroes. We lost a few at home in the war on drugs as well. At war, wearing uniforms, in Vietnam and other spaces. Conflicts at home and abroad, that some were privy to live through.

POEM

By Baba Jamal

There is a magic in the air, intentions hard to bear
Potential everywhere
It's our time to pick up
A cross to bear the
Regaining neighborhood,
Some the same, here and there
Where young Ancestors stood
It's family ties
It's still I rise
It's Spirit and Prayer
Deposited everywhere
Here – North, East, South, and West
May our memories sadness and JOY
Our challenges and families
Our families and our friends
Reunite in spite, and when and where

We can, Winbrook Pride will always exist,
Wherever and However, We Stand

Baba Jamal:

Remembering Because We Never Forget: White Plains

Carver Center on Main Street, Bly Sweater from 125th Street in Harlem, New York City. Supported by some "kicks" (shoes) from Delancey Street in downtown Manhattan. Supported by caddying 18 holes, on weekends, and rolls of 5 a.m. paper delivery with my brother-in-law. Financing clothes to be worn on Main Street at the Carver Center Rec, with special friends dancing to special songs, with special feelings, with teenage energy and everlasting love, that was truly understood. Even when we moved to H.L. Greens upstairs with an early curfew in a new foster home. God Bless and Rest in Peace, those who are gone, and some who live on. Everyone who cared about a young man born with no home to call his own. Aunties, Sisters, Mothers and Brothers, and homes are gone, but the Love lives on...The "Love" lives on...The Love Lives. Amen. You hear me, Lorenzo...And God Bless, Eugene and Gary. Y'all know who you are...Don't let me start calling names and places. I was a village child. May all my brothers and sisters hear me now ...Love and Blessings! Back to Winbrook, where track races were held around the circle. Girls and Boys. And who was that sister from 33 that no one could beat? It was 33, wasn't it? Some runners up in that house!

Memories that last forever....

Brenda Vinson recalls: "My family lived in 135 South Lexington. I remember turning all the lights out in the stairway from the 9th floor down to the first floor, playing tag on roller skates, from early summer mornings until breezy night... Ms. Shay, in the Big Playground, doing arts and crafts ...so much more..."

Jan Mayzack - remembers the kids playing hide and go seek in the circle when she was growing up. There were several social spots of note: There was, of course, H. L. Greens, The Epsilon for the older crew, The Ambassadors for the younger crew, Esaw's, and the Ink Spot where everybody hung out on Lexington Avenue, just to name a few.

Joe remembers:

Weekends often found us at either the Carver Center, Saxon Woods, or in the playground with an occasional trip to Rye Playland if we were lucky. Some of the older brothers sometimes would even find a way to get themselves into H. L. Greens, a local nightclub on Friday nights. This is where I stuck my head in the door one Friday night while "Patty La Belle and The Blue Bells" were performing but was quickly escorted out when they noticed I was too young to be there. The Cage Rec Center and later, The Slater Center also became places folks could gather to hang out and have fun.

Baba Jamal Reflects:

And who was that little snot head at the new Fisher Avenue Basketball Court that took my legs out on my way to a dunk? I was up in the air and came down on both of my wrists and one knee. I ended up spraining both wrists! I hope he missed every shot he took ever in life and that he never grew tall enough or strong enough to dunk on a regular-sized basket or basketball! LOL (I know…that ain't funny. Just kidding). Bless him for the experience, and the lesson…everything for a reason …and what? Yes, yes… and a season. God Bless us All!

Baba Jamal - remembers the day a young girl named Linda from 11 Fisher Avenue got hit by a car in front of the building. Everybody was stunned by all the blood we saw on her leg, but she managed to survive.

Wilbur Rooke "Dune Bug" - recalled that drugs started coming into Winbrook around 1965. He remembered all the Block Parties and going to H. L. Greens and hanging out at Saxton Woods.

Valerie Simmons – I believe Lena Anderson was the first African American Cheerleader. In subsequent years, Jennifer Colle followed, as did my sister Trina Simmons, who became team Captain. Sandra Rooke and others followed after that. White Plains High School had two marching corps: the Tigerettes which selected girls who were 5'4" in height and taller. Gail Hamilton, Sandra Simmons, Pat Mines, Yvonne Jackson, Joan Hadley, Andrea Clark, and many others were part of this group. The Bengelettes were the other group for girls of shorter stature. Gail Mines and I were selected for this group as were many others; and unfortunately, I dropped out after two years to take an after-school job. Others that followed included Debbie Reed,

Geraldine Mack, and again - many others. Can't forget the Twirlers – Virginia Mebane was Captain, Cheryl Martin, Laurie Salley, Leonarda Townes, and Sandra Hull were all on that same team. The main theme here is young ladies from Winbrook began infiltrating and passing the criteria and selection process for these groups.

Joe remembers the Dirty Dozen:

They were a group of girls that patrolled the area and kept everything in check. This group was originally called "F Troop" and was headed up by one of the sisters from 135 named Nita Roper, who I came to know, and her sister Francis, as friends in the Winbrook community. They later became known as "The Dirty Dozen," I don't know how they got the name, but I know they weren't to be messed with or taken lightly. Even the brothers in the neighborhood gave them their space and showed them respect.

Joe recalls:

In addition to starting at Rochambeau and Post Road Elementary, Eastview, Highlands, and Battle Hill were the junior high schools that most, if not all, people attended but the true test of faith was when you finally arrived at the "high school," White Plains High. Yes, that was the pinnacle, everybody heard stories about what would happen when you got there. Everything from "you would get beat up on the first day" to "you would meet new friends and have a great time!" It was possible that both could be true, but the suspense was always there. White Plains High had a good reputation in Westchester County academically and was well respected in all sports but was known especially for football, basketball, and track. Joe remembers the swim team having only one Black student, a brother from the projects named George Sessoms. George was a good athlete. I don't think he played any other sport, but man did he love to swim. It was his thing.

More Places and People in Our Winbrook Memories…

Who Knew Who?
Baba Jamal

Before we start, let it be known that Baba Jamal, a.k.a. Looney, or James, was a member of "The Disciples" a social club, and not a gang. He joined in its waning years. "I didn't have a pretty sweater like some of the others, but they let me in. The only real memory I have of its short life is going to the amusement park in Rye, representing who we were. Some had on the official sweaters, others didn't. But we still swaggered around the Park. We were treated with respect. If we saw a stranger, one of the homeboys may have let him slip to set him up with another local who may have a different approach to dealing with strangers." "What's up my man?" "Say ain't you Looney's cousin?"

If he just kept walking and just looked straight ahead, we probably just said some words that he could hear, as long as, he kept on walking. Depending on whether, or not some trouble was going on, that would probably indicate whether he was left alone, or somebody rolled up on him again, or… It all depended on the atmosphere, or if one of them wanted to prove something. It could also be a different situation like when those bloods from New Rochelle showed up the day after one of their boys was stabbed at a White Plains versus New Rochelle Football game. The night before, at the stadium, a brother from the Valley got caught up in some activity, and a New Rochelle brother was also stabbed.

"The next thing that happened, I felt like it was me, Kenny Mack, Willie Foster, and someone else from 159 approached the two carloads from New Rochelle (was it "Coon?"). It took a few minutes after they pulled up before we approached, but after we talked a while, more brothers from the buildings lined up. They were informed that the brother involved in the fight was in a solo situation between him and their boy, and that, that boy was already arrested. They cooled down after hearing that, and some of us started making connections with some of them."

That's what we remembered, having been remembered, and we're sticking to it! This was before I hooked up with my adopted cousin Luis Bahamunde, whom I met in downtown Manhattan. That's another story.

"Speaking of stories, there was that party in Elmsford when Tiggy had to give a boxing lesson. It was me, Hank, Ozzie, Tiggy and one other (Willie?). We know there were five, cause that's how many the Studebaker could hold! We all were dancing with the sisters, and I was dancing with this one sister, and this particular brother didn't like it, so he pulled out his knife. "Come on, you're supposed to be so bad. I heard about you. Come on!" "Put the knife down and let's roll!" This went back and forth until the local brothers started gathering, so Tiggy pushed me out the way, and hurt that other brother with about four punches. We turned around and hauled it and jumped into the Studebaker in a Cool kind of way, but hauling, nonetheless. I said, "I had him ok," Tiggy said, "Yeah, but you were taking too long to get him!" Ossie said, "I thought Loon' was going to talk him to the ground." Everybody started laughing, talking about each other. On the way back to White Plains, we all laughed at how each of us responded when the Elmsford crew started gathering. Tiggy, Ozzie, Hank, and me. There may have been one more. I think it was Willie. What a memory. Oh, and there were no real repercussions either. I had three of four sets of cousins, and a few other family friends in Elmsford, so everything was cool. But look, I sure was glad Tiggy was there with his talents!"

We may all have gone our separate ways over the years, but family is family, however you describe it, or whether we accept it or not... Even if we've forgotten space, time, activity, and faces.

This is one for the Winbrook Memories Project - And look, they forgot that the Blood from Elmsford had a knife in his hand. Just saying (lol).

There was ALWAYS something happening in Winbrook. Either it was internal or external or even invasive activity. Fortunately, there was always someone around who could balance the negativity, or at least give it a good fight; and place it or get rid of it. A lot of things happened in our Winbrook "Village," so much so that certain folks had to step up and dismantle the negativity...from time to time. For example, there were always some ancillary folks that were close to, or who felt like they were close enough to the Winbrook Village to start or control some "mess." More often than not, this wasn't the case. If you didn't know the building-by-building hierarchy, chances are you weren't welcome at any time, at all. There was also some hit-and-run activity from time to time.

"Punk a…Moth…."

Valerie Simmons Interview - Summary

During her recorded interview, Valerie Simmons provides an in-depth look at life in and around Winbrook as a member of one of the first families ever to move into the apartments…33 Fisher Avenue…. when they were initially built:

Valerie started by pointing out that her family was among the first to move into Winbrook and that 33 Fisher Avenue was the first building in the development. She remembers at least two other families that moved in with them; Mr. Miles, the Lynks family, and two others she couldn't recall bringing the number to five. These were the first five Winbrook residents who started the whole process which continued to grow as other families moved in and the other four buildings were put in place, creating the foundation for what would later be known as "Winbrook Pride."

Valerie, recalling that Winbrook became the hub of the Black community in White Plains, remembers that the Winbrook community was beautiful, and the apartments were fantastic. She said, "The bathrooms, kitchens, and everything was so nice. You didn't realize what you had until you visited others as a teenager, some people were still living in cold-water flats." She remembers it being so desirable to move into Winbrook that many people applied. In the beginning, the criterion was that you had to be a veteran because they were the first ones to get approval, and her father was a veteran. You also had to be married so there were no single parents at first.

Valerie remembers:

There was so much good happening around Winbrook at the time because so much of the area had African American businesses and a lot of Jewish businesses. It was all one big family, even some Italian businesses were there as well, and you could leave your doors unlocked because the neighborhoods were safe. We had relay races around the big circle in front of 33. In the summer there were tournaments, relay races, and when we got older it was just a nice gathering place for everyone from the Valley, the Hill, and all over. A lot of talent came out of Winbrook, and it was a friendly meeting place. The Hill was Ferris Avenue, the Valley was down in the Kensico area and Lake Street. The circle was there from the very beginning along with the benches and the little stores right across from Fisher Avenue.

Valerie recalled the Williams family from 33 Fisher Avenue who Joe knew well. We called Ms. Williams the Laundry Lady and she had a daughter, Pearl, who was her only child. You could always buy your bleach from the Laundry Lady. Oh yes, the laundry room was a fabulous place; the extraction machine, I was so scared of it. It cost an extra dime, but it would take out all the moisture. Joe pointed out that Ms. Williams was well respected in the Winbrook community and her daughter, Pearl, was good friends with his little sister, Lil. Joe's mother was the home care nurse for Ms. Rowells, an elderly lady who lived by herself on the 9th floor and that's how they got to know the families at 33. Ms. Rowells' son, Clayton, was an actor who lived in New York City and he would come up to see his mother from time to time.

This takes Valerie to her memories of the Evans family:

Ms. Williams and her family lived on the first floor next to the Evans family. Our families shared circumstances; we lost our mother when we were young, and they lost their mother when they were young....so our fathers kept us together. Our fathers raised us, and everybody respected Buddy Simmons. If youth gathered in the lobby hallways, which was against the Management rules, there was always a "look-out" for my father - someone would yell out "here comes Mr. Simmons" and we would run like the wind. Proud to say he was our self-appointed police officer. This brings to memory that Martin Rogers, Glenn Rogers' father, became the first black Police Officer hired in White Plains.

Valerie reflects:

The Evans sisters of 33 Fisher, I wish I could have brought one of them here today. They are like my other sisters. Out of that family, three of the sisters ended up becoming schoolteachers in the White Plains school system, and one of them became the first Black principal of Post Road School. I also remember Lerone Evans. Then you had others like Malcolm Graham, he was an NBA basketball player who played for the Celtics and became a judge in Massachusetts after he retired...we had so many people we connected to growing up in Winbrook...several success stories...a number of them.

Valerie continues:

Great things came from our buildings in Winbrook, like the Lynks (our other adopted family); the youngest brother, Rahku, is now a karate Sensei. And his sister Lillian was one of the first Black students to be accepted into the program where you go overseas to school as a foreign exchange student. She went to Switzerland to study, she is now in Chicago, and she became a professor. The whole family is very, very talented. Ella Jean, her third sister, is in NJ, she became a schoolteacher, and now she is a minister. Barbara Lynk was a lifeguard at the little playground, sadly; Barbara made her transition a few months back. She was a stunner to look at, all those girls were very attractive.

Valerie remembers a young brother from 33 being the first one to pass away from an overdose. I'll never forget that. Baba Jamal recalled the event and remembers that he and Freddie Mack tried to get him some help that night.

Valerie discussed isolated kinds of events and areas people couldn't go to in surrounding communities:

"I didn't feel that actually until we were, I would say, in the early first desegregation ahead of its time. I think because we went to Rochambeau and from Rochambeau, we went to Post Road, and then we went to the Highlands and then to High School. However, my younger siblings were at Post Road, and then they got shifted off into broadened desegregation. North Street School, Ridgeview (what did we know about that?) we just knew what was in our community. We loved walking to school with our friends, then they started busing, and that's when my younger siblings went to North Street School. A little different, but it still went well, and they didn't have any issues. Now I do remember in High School in '68 when we had the riots."

Joe recalled the first high school protests in 1968; demanding that Black History courses be added to the school curriculum. Then around 1970, another riot broke out at the high school. Students were kept outside of class for a period of time and some classes were taught at churches in the community.

Valerie reflects:

Oh yes, I was running around, I found my sister and told her "Leave the classroom, we are rioting."

Classes had to be held in the churches. I believe Trinity was one of them, something called the "Freedom Schools" was formed and we were able to continue getting our education that way

Because we were under curfew, I remember the guys from Silver Lake, they were coming around shooting; this was the scariest time.

We had classes at the Freedom Schools on Saturdays, and we had a group of students who met with the school board. We were instrumental in having those racist sons of guns from Silver Lake removed. We challenged that; we said no more. Whoever was there would be allowed to graduate and then they cut it off at that point, they could no longer attend school.

Baba Jamal pointed out during the 1968 protest-- We used to have our annual throw down on the front lawn, but we didn't do it that year because once the activity started, we were all vocal about our demands. There was a truce called, and I remember us all being in the auditorium... Glenn Rogers and the Chinese student named Fox, along with James Myers, our spokesmen. Many people didn't know it, but I was the invisible 4th man.

Baba Jamal continues: And while they were meeting in the auditorium somebody came to me, I forgot who it was and said who is this? What was the Pastor's name of the church on the corner? His son was a big-time singer - Amos? This was right near the campus and a whole bunch of riot gear showed up. What was surprising is that I was coming home from the Valley the week before late one night and saw all of that equipment being brought into White Plains; it was just like a caravan of police and everybody was under curfew. I remember the guys from Silver Lake coming down with guns. This was quite serious.

Joe pointed out that during one of our earlier trips home to conduct interviews, Baba Jamal and I were told by the director of the library a formal study had been done about the protests at White Plains High in 1968. That was something we didn't know but glad we were able to see a copy of the research and findings from this study at that time.

Valerie concluded:

Yes, that was big, so big that it got a lot of us into our African history. White Plains was ahead of the curve They brought those classes in the following year and developed a better rapport with the students. We needed more African American teachers and still struggled with that, but it was more promising than before.

Memories surfaced during the interview of Winbrook folklore such as the brother from 135 named Buckus, yes, Smith in 135, wise for his age. He was said to be the first to throw a football onto the top of one of the buildings. Valerie said his sister, Sharon Smith, was her age and now lives in the Poconos. She remarried but was first married to Chucky Seward, Bahru's cousin who is now a Karate Master in White Plains.

Valerie said the races around the circle and the fun they had in the little playground were unique.

We had the little playground; therefore, we wouldn't go to the big playground at certain times. We were just too young.

There was the Blue Building. Many referred to it as the "House of Soul". I remember chaperoning parties and my dear friend Jackie Evans-Roberts and Holland Randolph were heavily involved with programs for the youth!

Valerie also recalled the changes when a slow transition of drugs began to infiltrate the community: It was a slow process. I remember the transition when the drugs infiltrated. I remember when my father took on five guys in the hallway, he had like a cut, and I was ready to grab a knife and get whoever hit my daddy. I was ready and it was time for us to move. Circumstances made it difficult for large families or any family for that matter to move, but after this incident, I said, "Dad, we have to make a move." It took a little time, but we finally moved thereafter.

Valerie remembers:

As different things happened with public housing management. I remember the first woman who moved in that was unmarried. Then they were allowing more poor people to come in under certain circumstances, even when I worked for public housing. A woman down in Lake Street complained; "They wouldn't let me in because my husband and I were divorced." People were scared to go into the management office. Oh, it's just like this stuff shouldn't come to his office. I always said I wanted to work there, and people shouldn't have to come into the office afraid to talk or bring up a problem. I had a cousin that worked there as well. It was a scary place, like a prison, and wasn't very receptive. I said, when I got hired, I knew what it was from within, so I had to change that. You had to know how to let the people understand what's right and what's wrong. They may not like it but you should talk to them about it in a civilized manner so they would understand.

Valerie's thoughts on what kept the community together:

It was just family and extended family. I was over there at 159. My father said I shouldn't go, but I did. It wasn't the building; it was the things on the street; all that traffic. He wanted us to stand where he could see us. We had two-way streets back then, 159 was two-way and so was Grove St., all of that. We had big parades, big Thanksgiving parades; all we had to do is go to the parking lot of 33 and sit in front of 225. We saw the beginning of the parade and it was fabulous. Back then the community was connected, so if you did something wrong your parents would know before you got home. Yes, interconnected ...

As a community ....my older sister said, "Oh yeah, I didn't get to go to college, but I graduated from Winbrook U, our own university." That's how we learned a lot from each other -- we took so much pride in Winbrook. We still take pride in it. Some people today say they won't walk through there, but I will. I took pride in Winbrook; it was my home.

Joe shared, "I came home with my son who graduated years later --we walked through the Winbook community just to reminisce. Walking past all the buildings and going through what used to be the circle brought back memories for both of us, my generation and his."

Valerie reflects:

I still run into people like Rose Jamison. Why can't we have a reunion? Well, somebody has to help us. We should do it, but I can't do it by myself. There's somewhat of a reunion when we run into people at somebody's funeral, usually at Bethel, but that's not how it ought to be. She recalled the kind of events that made the community more cohesive--you know, special events that occurred...some things that were spontaneous such as the summer relay races were something we all looked forward to. Back then, we couldn't barbecue -- so it was a big thing when we packed up and went to the big parks. Families would meet there but, other than that, there wasn't too much, but you can never forget the Show Mobile and the fabulous artist they had singing songs! Also, going to the recreation park roller skating, ice skating— recreation was crucial. The Carver Center dances everybody wanted to go to. Sometimes people would catch me, and my father would get me out of there. The original Carver Center was located on Main Street, and under urban renewal then moved to North Lexington Avenue. Once the renewal project encroached down North Lexington, the Carver Center was no more- the fight began to establish Slater Center.

Joe pointed out that was also around the same time his brother's karate school would hold these big demonstrations at the park up on Ferris Ave. breaking ice, bricks, and everything, putting on a show for the community. They also established the Carver Center temporarily in the Big Blue Building on Fisher Ave. where my brother taught his karate classes for a while in the '70s.

Valerie Reflects:

It was in the '70s, I was happy so many people started taking Karate with him because it gave them such good discipline. We needed that. I remember giving out free lunches in front of 33, that was one of my first little jobs working with the kids. I remember joining a Black Panthers group with the free lunches and all. Eddie Hull from 135 got into that and my father came home, and he said, "My job knows you are trying to get into that --I can't lose my job," so that was it.

Joe and Jamal both reflected on the JABO boycotts of certain stores to protect the rights of people in our community and keep them from being taken advantage of.

Valerie acknowledged it probably did --a lot was going on. Urban renewal came in right after that -- it took all the Black businesses away. My father took me to City Hall --In City Hall, even today there is a three-dimensional thing of what was planned and what Winbrook was supposed to look like. Winbrook was always five X's, I'll never forget that. Later they put up a little building, but at first, it was just the five X's. My father said he knew they wanted to make it "White" Plains. My grandfather had his first Black cab company. Then he and my father bought a gas station, so we needed to know how to manage it. We didn't know we had to get gas to put in the big tanks, when the gas ran out, we had to keep filling it up. It was the gas station on Lake Street. It's still there, the BP station is what it's called now.

Jamal asked of any other kind of association with the other communities in the area like in the Valley or up on Battle Hill, any kind of cohesiveness with Fisher Ave, or feelings of that sort of thing you remember?

Valerie responded, "I think when we had the riots at the high school that brought us together. Unfortunately, there was always a rivalry between the Valley, even with the girls in Winbrook. If there were a block party or something like that, it would bring people together. We did ourselves a disservice, though, because we segregated ourselves. I live in this area; you live in that area and you all are from the projects; none of us could really be together. I always found that even with the churches, everything was apart. That's my personal opinion and there was nothing to bind us as a community. Up to recent times when Mr. Chamberlain was killed in 135, we got together in Slater Center and I couldn't believe there was no Black turnout. This happened in our community, where were all the people? There were more white people there than Black people. After all this buildup and national headlines about the police shooting, there was no real sense of community."

Joe pointed out that was not always the case. During the mid-1960s in the days of the JABO protest, the community turned out in large numbers to support any 'cause' that came up in Winbrook and around the city. There was once a community meeting held in the Fisher Avenue Carver Center building that had a Black turnout of over a hundred people to protest racism in the White Plains Taxi service and to boycott their operation. Joe Mack and James Coram played a key role in these events.

Joe pointed out there was also a time when the community tried to support Ms. Harry from 135 in her activities. It seems she was trying to represent people who were having trouble paying their rent and so forth when she confronted the housing authority.

Valerie recalled Ms. Harry – well, she was a spokesperson for welfare rights, that was her main cause. Unfortunately, she lost a lot of support because of some personal family issues. We undercut ourselves in that regard because she was a voice to be reckoned with in our community. Her boys were smart as a whip, brilliant guys. I went to school with Warren. Things just didn't work out well for them.

Valerie recalled memories of Willa Waller, her Big Sister mentor. Willa grew up in 135. After Willa graduated from college, she returned to her community and became a mentor to dozens of teenage girls. Willa was the brainstorm to develop the original Big Sister Program, sponsored by the YWCA in White Plains. Big Sisters became so talented in African Dancing, African Fashion, and Drama, that we were invited to perform in other school districts, including in Harlem. We had an invite for our dancers to join in with the famous African Drummer Baba Olatunde – and we were excused from our own school time to do so! I became the Fashion show coordinator, designing, sewing all outfits, and choreographing the models for the walkway. Back then, we didn't know much about HBCU schools, and Willa coordinated trips to many of the historically black colleges/universities to expose us to a whole new world. It was a beautiful time, that has afforded beautiful memories. I love you, Willa, along with your sidekick Sandra Bowen for all you did to help me and so many others see our full potential. Winbrook needed more of you. The original Big Sister group has now morphed into a new adult composition that plans to pass along enhanced mentorship to young ladies in need. There are so many athletes to recall, a few I admired from 33 were Mal Graham, Dave Jackson, Angus Corley, Carl Reed, Bob Jenkins, Darryl Turner; countless others from other buildings, and of course Eric and Clifton Livingston from 159, but none so fast and furious as Earl and George Rainey from 225, along with Ronald Moss.

We still get together when we can. I understand they have a newer group now with the Big Sisters, but the original Big Sisters, it was a Big Sister and a Little Sister program, that was us, can't take that away from Willa Waller. Sandra B. Jenkins came in underneath Willa with that program. The Rainey brothers were fine and great athletes, and we had so many others.

Joe remembered the African Dance troupe performing at Westchester Community College when he was President of the African American Society as well, during a program called "Black Day on Campus" --- a spectacular performance that topped off the entire program!

Valerie then reflected on extended families:

The Mines family from 225 – our parents were such good friends that they participated in each other's wedding party. We remain super tight to this day. Closest of ties with the Lynks, Reeds, Evans, Smalls, our 3rd-floor neighbors - the Clow family. I remain close with my Caucasian sister Barbara, the Bennetts of 11, and countless more. Theresa Jenkins and Ada Jackson were great mentors. Tee still refers to me as her "Lil Sister".

After our mother's passing in 1966, David Jackson's mother stepped in as a surrogate Mom. It was time for my Junior High prom, and Mrs. Jackson took me for my first shopping experience at Lord &Taylor in Eastchester to purchase my prom outfit.

Aunt Mimi, Aunt Regina, Aunt Emma, and Aunt Gerri were always available. Percy and Uncle Billy provided car rides to and from high school.

Valerie also recalled the Rudd brothers – all three became instant big brothers after our mother's passing. It's that sense of community that I love recalling and have tried my best to put into action with others.

I remember the Rudd brothers, they were just kind and looked out for us, everybody looked out for everybody. The Reeds: Carl, Jimmie, all of them are gone. We were the anchor families of Winbrook. The large families, the Johnsons in 159, Pat Johnson, Linda Johnson. There were so many I can't remember all of them. The Hulls, the Hadleys, the Heath family…

Jamal pointed out that we saw each other in school and after school. In a way, it was a sense of looking out for each other for a long time… "Who would you like to see again?" Valerie responded, "Kathy Reed aka "Kaky" has transitioned, I'll see her in another life – I miss her terribly."

Valerie: I see quite a few, unfortunately, during funerals. I'd like to see the Grahams again. We still stay in touch with the families we are close to, which is a great thing.

Jamal asked what was the change and what brought that in?

Valerie: And then it came –the change was gradual through urban renewal. What happened was they built the first affordable co-op, Summit House, on Ferris Avenue. A lot of families left, the Hunts, which our family was close to, and other families that became "over-income" because remember, Winbrook families that could afford to move out did move out. Unfortunately, many of the families that moved in did not take pride in where they lived and were not living by the rules. The transition came with people living on fixed incomes, maybe welfare, and those that were not from the community. People lost touch with each other, families who were close to each other, when they saw these outsiders coming in said, "Like, why are they moving in, where are they coming from?" We lost so many of the original families because it was time for them to move on. As their income went up, it forced families to move. Winbrook back then was under the control of the state and became federal in 1982, that's when I was hired. Under state control, you could get fined if you walked on the grass. Remember we had the little chain link fences? We respected that but when it became federal the fine system went away--nobody's respecting anything anymore. After it became federal, they would say "We can't be fined, it's under federal control now." So, if you wanted to fine someone you had to organize the residents and they had to issue the fines themselves. That wasn't going to work, that was an impossibility, and for 36 years I tried to get it across to them it would never work. What happened next, you built 86 Dekalb Avenue and the Lake Street apartments which became part of White Plains housing and I didn't know that I only knew Winbrook.

When I was hired, I found out it was for Lake Street and DeKalb and I learned everything was under federal control.

Then you had the renovations that were a nightmare. You can't move people like that, we're not animals--throwing stuff on the truck, and things were flying off the truck, no this is not working. They went from one apartment to another, during the first renovations they gave everybody a new shower, a new kitchen, this and that, but it wreaked havoc because you didn't see the whole picture.

You have to remember, when we were growing up, we had the incinerator, no bugs, no mice, nothing because everything got burned. Then ecology awareness happened, and you have to close it down--now we had a compactor and that was a whole different ball game. A different approach should have been put in place to relay pertinent information to the residents. Failure to do that resulted in residents' mistrust and non-compliance. Between the change in the government status and the change in management, people were losing respect for the management, and the manager wasn't trying to help people. They weren't communicating with people.

People weren't meeting with each other. When I got the job, I said, "You know you have resident rights; you need to form something, stop coming down here to complain and do something as a group. I'll help you out, I'll put my stuff on the line, but I'll help you."

Folks were isolating themselves, leading to weakened friendships, creating fewer community interactions and oversight of the Winbrook complex. The blending comradery of five buildings was dissolving. Former well-established neighborhoods uprooted via urban renewal – known as Urban "Removal" were shifted from one area of town to another. The newly formed communities of 120 Lake Street and 86 DeKalb became more fragmented from Winbrook.

In recent years development of new building replacements at the Winbrook site, the new dynamic now includes admission of many new families, with many having no familiarity with White Plains. New names are in place for each new building replacement- The Prelude, The Overture- no more building numbers. Even the name of Winbrook will be no more. Thank God for the good memories.

Valerie pointed out that when the new building transition began, Winbrook residents had priority. It was all Winbrook people who got to move in first, but they had to go by a lottery system, it was the only fair way to do it. A lot of people who were chosen for the lottery didn't take it because they were afraid of the change. Now, after the new people moved in, they said, "Oh can I get in?" It was too late. The lottery system got you in. Look how long it's been since 135 has been closed and you can't get it knocked down because of asbestos. You have all the courthouses and the churches in the vicinity, you can't just implode the building. It's like you'd have to disassemble that building almost brick by brick. Do you know how much money that is going to cost? They are in a snag and now you have the federal administration that won't give you a doggone dime so they're in a quandary. I am so happy I retired.

And now they are saying White Plains Hospital is going to creep in--who knows because if they don't get the money they can't sustain, they can't. HUD was a big cash cow, about 20 years ago I knew it was gonna happen. I was telling the residents; they've got to get themselves together. I could see it coming and they said, "Oh, they ain't gonna do nothing because they're all under federal control."

Jamal established there were issues of government interference or change in strategies; dope came in –

Valerie: It's still there- the selling of drugs and less of a focus on education...what happens next? You try to teach. From my time there I was trying to teach, and I did a little bit of that. People didn't know how to clean their stoves. We had to have apartment inspections every year, and that was one of my many tasks. I couldn't believe what I was seeing; there was no regard for turning off the TV or turning off lights because they didn't think they had to do that. So, I had to tell them, "Let's get educated here because sooner or later you are going to have to pay." Rent increases will become inevitable no matter what subsidy will be forthcoming via Tax Credit or Section 8 calculations. Prior renovations at Winbrook proved my point. During the initial Federalization upgrades in Winbrook during the early '80s, electric meters were installed in all units, and residents became responsible to pay a share of their own utility bills. Once installations were completed, you could see lights out thru-out Winbrook versus the complex being lit up like a Christmas tree. Time changes everything and our home communities have to be made aware and made ready for the adjustments and compliance – it's life.

Valerie made the point that initially, there was always a waitlist-- up to the time I retired when we were open, the people would line up to get on the list. We'd have people from other projects, especially Yonkers and Mount Vernon, trying to get here because they knew White Plains, as a whole, was a beautiful city to live in, if you could afford to live there and if you can get into someplace affordable, and that's the operative word--if. People weren't qualified because the screening process became tighter and more restrictive. At one point we were mandated to take in the homeless, had to --so that brought things down a lot. We had families we didn't know and didn't have to process all that well, but we had to take them.

Valerie closed with the good that came out of the Winbrook years: I think more good than negative came out of those years. It just never was put out there. Before I retired, for 30 some years or so I posted positive news articles from local papers on my massive bulletin boards, hoping to provide a feel-good moment and a sense of pride to the residents. So, when I retired, I sent positive articles to certain families and they were so appreciative--I said, "You hated my guts, but I waited for this day and I'm giving you a present (Joe interjects: How you like me now?) …how you like me now?" That's your family history, it was a positive event, and it was published in the paper, which our folks don't read that much. I realized that during annual inspections of units, not seeing books, magazines, or other reading materials displayed in quite a few homes – I believe my small gift of passing on news articles was much appreciated and made me feel good too.

Jamal: Something's going down nationwide, and I believe it's going to be the simple things, simple but necessary and important. I think that is what we should be emphasizing in our words and our writings. We want to thank you, and we're just happy you came.

Valerie: I want to thank you too, I'm so glad my brother, Glenn Rogers, sent your notice to me. We go back a long time.

Jamal: We're going to use this information and responses you have given us to put together if we can, something to enlighten, to make folks feel proud about Winbrook--just to have a record we were here and ---

Joe: It wasn't all bad---

Valerie: It wasn't all bad.

Valerie Simmons and Baba Jamal "The StoryMan" during her interview for the book
- White Plains, NY Library photo 2019

Following her interview, Valerie Simmons provided the following newspaper articles as documented evidence of the beginning stages of Winbrook and the families that first moved in:

NEWS ARTICLES:

Reporter Dispatch Saturday, July 22, 1950

1st Winbrook Tenants Move in Next Week

The first tenants will move into Winbrook Apartments, the first low-rent project of the White Plains Housing Authority, next week and a "house-warming" ceremony will be conducted July 31 by State Housing Commissioner Herman T. Stitchman.

Building No. 1, on Brookfield Street near Post Road will be filled first. It includes the heating plant. Building No. 3, Grove Street, and Building No. 2, Fisher Avenue, and Brookfield Street will be ready next, in that order. Later two more 90-family units will be built on the site.

The apartments will include a coin-operated laundry, with 16 machines and four extractors which will deliver clothes ready for ironing. There will be no outside clothes lines at Winbrook.

No outside television aerials, either on the roof or projecting from windows, will be allowed. Tenants may have television sets with inside aerials.

Garbage disposal will be handled by incinerator chutes on each floor.

In selecting tenants, preference was given first to site tenants, and second to war veterans according to degree of housing hardship, such as split families, evictees, etc.

Reporter Dispatch July 25, 1950

First 24 Families to Move Into Winbrook in Next 6 Days

Two White Plains policemen and one fireman will be among the first to move into the Winbrook Apartments project of the White Plains Housing Authority this week.

Mr. and Mrs. Thomas II Miles and one child of 29 Fisher Avenue will be the first to occupy a Winbrook apartment.

Pt1. Joseph Gaffney and Fireman Kenneth Henderson will move into Winbrook Thursday. Pt1. Bernard Seit will occupy an apartment Friday. All now live on South Lexington Avenue, on the site.

The uniformed men qualify and are high on the priority list, as site tenants, war veterans, within the income limits, and housing hardship cases.

Others on List

Others scheduled to move the first day are: Richard Hazelwood, 62 Winchester Street; Thomas Cartwright, 43 Winchester Street; John Simmons, 165 South Lexington Ave; Mattie Majors, 62 Winchester Street; James Smith, 288 Brookfield Street; John Hopkins, Greenburgh, but formerly of White Plains; Hardy Davis, 290 Brookfield Street; and Hollis Eisner, 271 Brookfield Street.

To move Thursday are: George Lohse, 97 Orawaupum Street; Frances Ceasar, Brookfield Street; Irene O'Heir, Walter Hurrelman, Josephine Thomas, Peter Crumin, Pt1. Gaffney, Anthony Orovich, Charles Miller and Fireman Henderson.

THE PATHFINDERS CLUB:

Valerie Simmons also provided us with a copy of a news article from the 1930s which identified her father, John Simmons, as one of the early leaders of an organization to support Black youth in the White Plains community called The Pathfinders Club. This is clear evidence that long before the Winbrook apartments were even built, there were those in the community who made an effort and the sacrifices necessary to lay the groundwork and example for the rest of us to follow. John Simmons was one of those people, as the following article describes, instrumental in the founding of the "Pathfinders Club."

Daily Press (White Plains) 1933

Our Westchester Clubs

The Pathfinders Club Offers Recreation, Service, Dignity (by Bill Haggins)

White Plains

In the beginning of White Plains history, there were many Indians, and after many years there came "Pathfinders', those who blazed trails through virgin forests and unknown country. The pathfinders marked trails followed later by the frontiersmen and trappers, next the pioneers, and then the settlers whose homes grew into villages, towns and finally today's cities.

But before all others went the pathfinders.

The Pathfinders Club of White Plains, Inc. fills this role for our community in Westchester. They own a private establishment here that strives to offer the dignity one would expect in his own home, emphasizing a wholesome refreshing atmosphere that would create the kind of enjoyment that all are asking.

Those responsible for this service to the community are John Simmons, president, Lindsey

Smith, vice-president, Thomas Lynde, treasurer, Frank Elleon, secretary and Joseph Alston, chairman.

As part of their program, they give up one of the most important nights of the week-end, Friday, to cater to our teen-agers, to give youth a chance to have a good clean place for recreation beyond reproach.

The hall is also rented for private parties, dances and weddings.

This year, the club is sponsoring a baseball club that is showing to be one of the best, and can be seen at Recreation Park, Sunday 2 P.M., May 19th when they take on Danbury, Conn. Public support of the team is one way of the community saying, "Thanks fellows, for all that you are doing."

And this reporter adds, "Why don't other clubs try to do something as wonderful too."

CHAPTER 3

ROLL CALL

Roll Call will reflect some of the names of people we knew who lived in one of the five buildings, as well as some of those who frequented Winbrook, with an occasional comment or memory related to that person. It is by no means a complete list and is certain to leave out some names or families simply due to lack of recall over the many years, but those we missed were indeed woven throughout the Winbrook experience and are embedded in our souls and spirits as well.

Reflections and Memories of Those We Knew:

The following is a result of Joe Mack and Baba Jamal brainstorming some of the people and names they could remember from in and around the five buildings:

Jamal: Who are we gonna talk about in this chapter Joe?

Joe: I've been toying with an idea, why don't we just list names that we remember off the top, and maybe even include situations, events, and activities.

Jamal: Ohh! I see. Kind of whatever comes to mind, let's write them down and see what we have.

Joe: Yes, yes, that's cool. Cause after that, we can also recall memories and events that folks we have talked with remembered.

Jamal: Sounds good to me Brother. We want to finish this project this year, for sure! Let's roll...

Remembering Some of The Brothers and Sisters, Families, and Friends, Who Came This Way:

Hopefully, we are not too late as we search our memories for friends, events, and residents of four major African American communities in White Plains, New York. We do so knowing that we have forgotten more than we remember and that we have "Strayed Away" too long. Hopefully, we have not lost all contact with those we love and care about. Those folks we call friends.

RECALLING PEOPLE - PLACES AND EVENTS

Personalities We Won't Forget: Who Lived in Winbrook
…and/or were seen there -frequently at all hours…

Folks We Remembered and Talked With that Lived in Winbrook
or Near Winbrook, or Had Relatives in Winbrook,
or Were in Winbrook Every Time You Turned Around,
And others who Had Nowhere Else to Go But,
Winbrook, the Valley, Ferris Avenue, Fisher Avenue

Here are some folks who called Winbrook Home 1965 and beyond. These names are listed in no particular order and the name of every member of a family may not be mentioned but you all know who we're talking about…

The Mines Family Pat - Rhonda, Gail, Jonette Karen, Dougie, Sarah – Jonette has become highly involved in community affairs and currently serves as Chair of the White Plains Juneteenth Committee.

Butch "Skeeter" Habersham - Had a scrape with a boy from Roosevelt HS in Yonkers.

The Howard Family (225 Grove) - Tony, Danny, Abe, Max, and Morris Howard

H.L. Greens - the dances upstairs on a Saturday night: Role Call - Abe Howard, Curtis Garner, Doug Williams, and others…and a hundred teenagers, waiting on a slow record…

Larry Branch - a sharp dresser who had the first portable telephone I ever saw.

The Simmons Family (33 Fisher) - Sandra, Trina, Valerie, Steve, Donnie, Donna, Tracey. Valerie worked with CAP and later as a Property Manager for the White Plains Housing Authority. The Simmons were among the first families to move into Winbrook.

The Daughtry Family (225 Grove) - Originally from Alabama.

Simon Jackson - dated Baba Jamal's cousin Debbie (33 Fisher)

The McLaughlin Family (159 S. Lexington) - Donnie, Andre, Jo Ann, and Mama McLaughlin. Baba Jamal met with Andre McLaughlin at Medgar Evers College in Brooklyn when The National Association of Black Storytellers had its festival a few years ago.

The Societies: R&B local Singing Group - George Young, James Coram, Darryl Cole, Earl Cole Jr., and others.

The Morgan Family (from the "Valley") - Alice, Charlie, Troy, Dennis. Dennis went on to play professional football for the Dallas Cowboys and several other teams during his professional career.

Ernest and Theresa Dimbo - Ernest was quiet but could hold his own on the courts as well. Much respect for this brother.

The Robinson Family – Pecola, Eddie, Mim, Jerome (Bump), Irving, Jonathan, Yvonne. Greg Robinson and Bobby Jealous connected in Johannesburg, South Africa. Jonathan married Valerie Hicks.

Jerome "Bump" Robinson -A "Legend" – What a difference he made in the communities of White Plains and in folk's lives. Wow! He was a Director WP Community Action Program, colleagues were Valerie Simmons Administrative Assistant, and Walter Bowen, Outreach Worker. Part of Ferris Avenue was renamed "Jerome Bump Robinson Way" to honor his memory.

The Lindsay Family (33) - Marvin, James, and Val. James "Snake" Lindsay graduated from Westchester Community College in Valhalla. A smooth brother and highly intelligent. The first from the Winbrook area to get a big-time job at

IBM when they were just getting established in Westchester County.

James Myers - Baba Jamal's Ace. He was the leader during the 1968 high school protest. Remembered him having house parties and us going down to New York on the last day of the World's Fair in New York City.

Billy Burton - Moved back to the Bronx and hooked up with the "Black Spades" Baba Jamal bumped into him and his "Crew" a block away from where Darryl and Winnie Cole were living. What a surprise! We greeted each other and he offered me: "If you need anything, just let me know, Looney." Much respect on both sides. Deltine Burton was his sister.

The Mack Family (159) - "4th Floor - More Macks but unrelated to the Macks on the 8th floor - Kenny Mack, Freddie Mack, Geraldine and cousin, Joyce Bryant. Freddie fought a good fight against an illness that led to medical treatment, but coming up he was a strong, quick brother. Kenny Mack Jr. went on to become a professional boxer like his father.

Clayton Rowells - He was a model for "Pomade Hair Grease" whose mother, Ms. Rowells lived in 33 Fisher.

Steve Washington - Played basketball at Westchester Community College in Valhalla, NY, and set the school's all-time scoring record of over 1,000 points by the time he graduated. His brothers were Skip and Rodney Washington.

Leroy "Buckets" Smith - rumor has it that one day he threw a football up to the top of building 33 Fisher!!! Some would say "man, that ain't no rumor...I was there!" What a feat, too bad he never got a look in the NFL.

Glenn Rogers - another of Baba's Ace and he was also a leader during the 1968 high school protest. Glenn married Katrina Simmons.

Artie Bennett - An awesome saxophone player from Winbrook who played in the many Show Mobiles around town and had his own jazz combo called "Mahaa." Artie went on to become known for his talents around the country and played for several impressive groups during his career.

Harold and George Williams. Their older brother was a policeman in White Plains who lived up off Fisher Avenue, on Lafayette Street. Their driveway backed up to Wyanoke St., the same street James Coram (yes, he did have an address! Lol), and Glenn Rogers lived on.

The Rudd Family (from the "Valley") - Larry Rudd, James Rudd, Timothy Rudd, Gloria Rudd, Timmy, and Charlie Rudd.

The Cole Family -Jennifer, Earl Sr. "Pops", Mama Elaine Cole, Darryl, and Earl Jr.

The Harry Family (135) - Warren, Jimmie, Mama Elsie Harry, and daughter Lynn

The Moore Family - Carolyn and Alonzo Moore

The Mitchell Family - George, Bae, and Jamorah Kai, and Tracy Wilson (niece) from 135 and the Valley (Lake St. Apts.)

The Harris Family – Doris, Benjamin, Gail, and Gwen (33)

The Williams Family – Dee, Gloria, Dougie, Dorothy, Gertrude Williams (11)

The Williams Family - Amanda "Pearl" Williams, Mama Williams, and Mr. Williams (33)

The Bennett Family – Ben, Jr., Karen, Renee, Debra, Adrian, Lisa, Eric, Derick, Leonard (159)

The Rooke Family – Ronald, Sandra, Wilbur, Ricky, Sharon, Linda, Paula, Michelle (159)

The Roper Family – Sam, James, Lewis, Lynda, Frances, Anita, Michael, Richard (135)

The Mack Family - "8th floor" - William, Joe, Lillie, Gamal, and Mama Mack (159)

The Holdip Family - Ricky, Ronnie, and Reggie Holdip (225)

The Roberts Family – Nate, Pat, Johnnie, Eddie, Eleanor, Winston, Reggie, Nancy, and sweet Mom Ms. Mary – giver of homemade goodies to all throughout the Winbrook complex (33)

The Jackson Family – Yvonne, Garfield "Stonehead," Mark, Renee Jackson (33)

The Higgs Family - Mama Higgs Otis, Leon (159)

The Sessoms Family - George, Judy (11)

The Livingston Family - Mama Livingston, Eric "Coon", Hasker, Gary, Clifton, Wilbur (159)

Livingston Twins - Warren and Stanley (135)

The Rhodes Family - Eric, Michael, Brenda, Jason, Elgin (135)

The Merrick Family – Reggie, Elaine, and older brother (159)

The Reed Family – Ben, Jr., Carl, Kathy, Jimmie "Rasheen", Brian, Debbie, Patty, Penny (33)

The Hull Family – Ed, Loretta, Michael, Louis "Gremlin", Brenda, Sandra (159)

The Moss Family – Ronald and Herb (225)

The Mosley Family – Harold, Jean, Lawrence, William, Dwight

and more - - lots, lots MORE!

Back to Roll Call:

Stephanie Coram

Joyce and Sharon Coram (Baba Jamal's sisters)

George Andrews

Barry Bennett

Martha Richardson

Cedrick Thomas

Eddie Roberts

Gail and Patricia Mines

Caleb "Tiggy" Lawrence

Ozzie and Raymond Mitchell

Curtis Gardner

Donnie Simmons

James Jackson

Other Personalities: That just came up. We have a relationship somewhere in the families …Be Blessed!!!

Laurie Salley	Henry Johnson
Janet "Wink" Walker	Ronnie Johnson
Billy Walker "Bus Head"	Freeman Fulton
Ronnie and Patricia Horton	Freeman Beville
John and William Dubois	Larry Brown
Joe Bullock	Chuckie Addison
Ronnie Vinson	James Walker
Al Lewis	Michael and Judy Williams
Glen Smithson	William Bryant
Foster Turner	Cliff Wiley
George Andrews (11)	Mr. Salley
Deborah Howard	Marshall James "Old Man"
Dennis Silas (Post Road)	F. Poe
Artie Jenkins	Dougie Walker

Harry Johnson	Ella and Butch Coram
Hank and John Cook	Pam Brey
Reggie Johnson	Willie, Jimmie and Wendy Foster
Louis and Samuel Bryant	Daryl Jenkins
Irving Caesar	Jan Mayzack
Monroe Bowser	Judy and Eddie Peterson
Wayne Smith	Otis Moore "Dinky"
Jeff Horton	George and Earl Rainey
Abraham (Abe) Jenkins	Judy and Sandra Valentine
Frank Fuller	Pat and Pam Hilliard
Donnie Howard	Herschel Jacob
Jared Walker	Cleo Daniels
Charlie and Earnest Saunders	Earl Brey
Johnny Randolph	Bill, Kenny, and Joyce Cain (33)
Butch Mabry	Thomas "Ice" Harrington
William Hill	Brenda Williams
Hardy and Raymond Davis	Thomas Jordan
Wendy Younger	Charles and Frances Bristol
Eddie Wynn	Doug Waller
Elizabeth, David Foster	Boisey Mindinghall
Doris Hicks	Larry Branch
Frank Barnes	Bobby and Rita Portee
Rita Attaway	James Myers
Cheryl Seward	George Peterson
Tyrone Potillo	Tex and Irene Jones
Mozella Davis	Victor Clark
Theresa Shoulders	Carolyn Ravenelle (33)
Bobby Jenkins	Willie Foster
Walter Sutton	Steve Bowman
Raymond "Frog" and Muriel Jordan	George Rivers
Morris "Cowboy" Green	Otis Bagley
Alden Mitchell	Ben Harris
Eddie and Bertha Adams	Charlie Sasser (from Ferris Avenue)

Marc Wilson

Surya Peterson

James Gibbs

Phillip Francis

Claudine White

The Garnett Family - Rueben, Ronald, Robert

Mary Hipp

Pamela Lee

Roderick Gray

James Greenhill

David Jackson

Monica Cartwright

Linda Smalls

Sandra Simmons

Lenny Capers

Robert Threat

Rhonda Mines

Charlie Francis

Leonard Seward

Bahru Seward

And More…So Many More…

CHAPTER 4

WINBROOK MEMORIES

More Experiences - The Legacy Continues

By Baba Jamal:

August 2019 White Plains, NY, the story continues:

Joe L. Mack and Jamal R. Koram, W.P.H.S., Class of 1968

Again, fifty-two years is a long time to carry a memory…but not as long as forever… and we are blessed to be able to carry those people, places, or events, and remembering is a sign of caring, or vice versa. We care therefore, we carry the memories of people, places, and times. The caring is either for ourselves or for all who were involved…

Some memories are easy to forget or to leave where they are. Others are not so easy. For example, each one of us can recall, right now, a person, or place or event, that we have either locked away, dealt with, or that we do not want or need to bring up, or, that we WANT to remember no matter what emotion it calls to the surface because there is something about that place and time that we understand. Some of us have discovered that it is best not to fight the past; or to create a space that deletes that "time." Others haven't reached that plateau. So, we just create a space for that person or event, or we do not, and just keep on keeping on. Like that. This publication is about Love, Happiness, Sharing, Remembering, and Enjoying the memory. We pray that we have succeeded. Peace and Blessings!

Playground Life:

Everyone enjoyed it, from the shed to the small basketball court, to the main court, where folks jumped over the fence because they were up next, where you were good, or you didn't play. These courts weren't to be confused with Fisher Avenue courts which eventually became a place for summer league, where this punk-ass youngster took my legs from underneath me en route to a dunk. I sprained my wrists and scraped my legs. I let him slide, but I think someone else took care of that for me.

Scrapes and Scraps. Hope and Caring:

Meanwhile, back at the projects in the Winbrook playground...

Hammy was shooting a pistol (pellet gun) at folks playing ball on the big court. I was up next and felt that there was something I had to say or do. "Yo Hammy, you need to stop firing that gun, man. There are little children, and folks on the court, and that gun could ricochet and hurt somebody for no reason…" He said, "You gonna stop me Looney, Crip?"

"I done seen you in action, and I know what you can do Hammy, but I'm gonna have to do something, and let the play fall where it falls…" I knew I couldn't come close to stopping him, but I also knew I had to do something since I opened my mouth. Also, those young ones were at risk. His older brother came to the playground right on time.

All the sisters were telling the older brother what Hammy was doing, and what I did and long story short, his brother humiliated him in front of everyone. And his threats to me simmered down when he realized I had some backup that he didn't want to mess with…few, if any folks would.

These brothers/friends of mine spoiled me. Whew! Thank Goodness! Cause my mouth was faster than my hands. Oh, I could go to work for a minute, just enough for someone to jump in and take the slack off me. Like Tiggy did that night in Elmsford, but that's another story. Fortunately for me, the older brother happened to be walking through Winbrook and saw the last part of the gun episode and did what big brothers do….

It was embarrassing in one respect, absolutely necessary in another.

But I wouldn't bet no big money on Looney... LOL. Unless it was someone with a bigger mouth than mine now, if that happened, he would be in trouble from "Jump Street" Bigger Mouth, Slower Hands. J.K.

Some also remember the day Joe Mack had a minor incident in the playground. All the fellas were standing around like we usually do after playing ball, just shooting the breeze and talking trash. Kenny "Pluck Em" Cain and Joe were good friends, Kenny was about 6' 6' and Joe about 6' 1', but both were good athletes. All of a sudden, Kenny says, "Joe, I hear you can box...let's see what you got," and the two of them started throwing light jabs and just showing off for the girls... nothing serious. But then Dougie Williams from the Valley comes over and says to Kenny, "Move out the way man, you ain't got nothing for Joe. Let me show you how it's done."

We're not sure if Dougie had ever seen Joe in action, but he rushed in with some hard right hands towards the head, only to find that Joe had slipped under his blows and hit him about 5 or 6 times in his ribs before he could even bring his hands back! Everyone was amazed and enjoying the action as both guys backed away and decided enough was enough, and it was wise to stop before anybody got hurt. That was the "way of the wars" in the Winbrook Projects playgrounds.

There were several major neighborhoods in White Plains: Winbrook (The Projects), the Valley, and Ferris Avenue. Battle Hill was another one, then west, outside of White Plains, you had Greenburgh and Elmsford, beyond that, it was Tarrytown and Ossining, and the Hudson River. Outside of those areas you were into other cities in Westchester, like Yonkers South/southwest (Charlie Chris - Bernard Toone basketball phenoms), Mount Vernon (a basketball powerhouse) to the south, New Rochelle and Mamaroneck to the southeast, Port Chester to the east, and Peekskill (Brickhouse/basketball) to the borderline north...

Each neighborhood had brothers and sisters with reputations. This included those of us who didn't live directly in those neighborhoods but is where we were welcome, and doors were open. I had at least three homes in Winbrook.

Not to overdo hospitality, and not to refuse standing invitations. The Robinson brothers, and their many cousins, were from Ferris Avenue, Ernest Dimbo and them. There was also a period when families from Winbrook, and those from Fisher Avenue, moved into the large, relatively new apartment building on Ferris Avenue.

We recall when the Coles and the Moore's, among others, moved to the "Summit House." The land was "Changing Hands" in the "Projects" and a few blocks from Warwick Village, up Fisher Avenue. The demolitions had begun; following were those second and third blocks up to Highland Avenue. It stopped during that time in that area. Nowadays, if you've been gone a long while, you won't recognize much, and you may not know that many from 135 South Lexington, along with my ace, Willie Foster, and Mama Foster are gone in the flesh, but not in Spirit. Love y'all.

RICK ROBERTS INTERVIEW:

Our next live recorded interview was conducted with Richard "Rick" Roberts who grew up in Greenburgh, NY but lived with his parents in White Plains for a while and is now an attorney and financial consultant in White Plains. Rick recalls the early years when there were several Black-owned businesses in the city, as well as the role of his father in the neighborhood just as the Winbrook community was coming of age.

He provides an interesting point of view, much of which he gained through his father, to the lives and times of folks in and around the Winbrook community. Here Rick describes the influences and the role his father played in his life growing up and the memories he left behind for him to cherish. Here we also find that the "numbers game" was played in Black communities throughout the country and White Plains is no exception. Additionally, this interview clearly defines the interconnection between the cities of White Plains and Greenburgh, NY.

Rick started by stating his desire to meet with us:

Rick: I've been looking forward to meeting with you for some time.

Baba: Well, that's a good thing brother --Joe and I were sitting one day, and it came to us that time, as usual, was fleeting. Not only time but disruption was taking place, all the neighborhoods were changing, the streets were changing, so we needed to catch at least some aspects of our lives and who was in it at that time, during every generation...but go ahead and share.

Joe Introduces the team - Baba Jamal Koram from Alexandria and Joe Mack from Richmond, VA, while sharing that they both grew up in White Plains and the Winbrook area.

Rick: I was born in White Plains, raised in Greenburgh--Woodlands High school, class of '71.

Baba: Seventy-one, I see. I would have been at Woodlands in the class of '68, but I moved to White Plains in '63.

Rick: You might remember my friend Jerry Rice then; he was from White Plains.

Baba: Vaguely remember that name, yeah there was Ronald from out of Greenburgh, but he was before you.

Rick: Ronald Watson, I knew him.

Baba: But talk about some things and highlights that are in your mind.

Rick: Well, as I mentioned, the thing that always comes to mind with me in White Plains has got to be my father, Doyle Roberts – Mister D- as he was known at the time. He and his friend, Tex, had a hand in the numbers game in White Plains for a long time and he used to have a dry cleaner on Brookfield Street. There was also a rooming house over there, and my mother, Evelyn Roberts, had a beauty salon, Evie's Salon, just up from Fordham Lumber Yard right on the corner of Martine Ave and Brookfield.

Subscript: The Numbers Game preceded the modern-day lottery and was played in communities all over the US. It was used in minority neighborhoods primarily as a means to make enough money to tide them over to the next paycheck and to help them buy groceries or pay their bills. The concept was simple - you pick three numbers and turn them into the "numbers runner" with a bet of 25 cents up to about two dollars, depending on how much you were willing to risk. If your numbers "hit" at the end of the day, you got a portion of the overall pot, which was determined by how many others hit that day. Everybody in the neighborhood respected the numbers game and especially carried a deep regard for the man in charge. In a way, he was looked at as a resource that was relied upon by many in his community.

Baba: There was actually a Lumber Yard? Now I remember, and there was an apartment building across the street from that, I guess, right on the corner.

Rick: Yes, there was an apartment building on that corner and a butcher shop diagonally across the street.

Baba: Right, because my Godmother lived in that apartment, she and my mother shared a place right on Martine Ave.

Rick: Down on the other end --my dad's stuff--the numbers running, was all between the lumber yard and Mt. Hope Church.

Baba: That is what you would call a full-fledged neighborhood!

Rick: Oh Yeah

Baba: So, when you visited the area at that time you established friendships in White Plains and what not.

Rick: Oh Yeah, I had friends in White Plains, the Rice's up on Midland Avenue, and a good friend of mine, a firefighter who passed away back in 1993, Warren Ogburn and Kenny Faulkner were people I knew.

Baba: Yes, people and relationships are always paramount. Highlight things that have changed as you look back on that time and that space and those friends as you look back when the change starts to happen.

Rick: Urban renewal

Baba: Urban renewal nasty name isn't it... When Urban comes in...

Rick: Everything changes

Baba: Urban renewal is the one that started it all.

Subscript: Urban renewal involved the relocation of many families in the city of White Plains during the middle the to late '60s. As the city began to grow and expand, wealthy entities from within and the surrounding areas needed the space for office buildings, malls, and government facilities. Urban renewal was the process by which the city managers identified these locations and notified the families living in them that their neighborhoods were being developed by the city and that they would have to find somewhere else to stay within the next four to six months or so.

Baba: When people started moving --Did your friends move in areas beyond the limits of the Greenburgh and Tuckahoe area?

Rick: Most of my friends were outside of the actual urban renewal area, but everything changed. Things that you used to do, places you used to go – H. L. Greens.

Baba: Right --upstairs --Do you remember those parties up there?

Rick: I was too young --I remember them vicariously through my cousins, Rene D'Arbeau and Teddy Selby, who used to come to my house or live with me or visit my folks from time to time, but the parties were a little bit before my time.

Baba: What about the center across the street down here in White Plains-- the Carver?

Rick: Yes, the Carver Center I used to go there sometimes.

Baba: Yeah, those were the opportunities that were available, if they could be called opportunities. I know you mentioned H.L. Greens, which was an outlet for young folks around White Plains. Carver was a different kind of thing. It was an exchange between Elmsford, Greenburgh, and White Plains, and a whole mix of things that created some of the highlights. Thinking of your childhood coming up, people you remember, and things that they did--I remember the Korver brothers from Greenburgh.

Rick: I remember the twins --don't even know their names, but I still see them.

Baba: What twins?

Rick: I met them playing basketball when they had urban renewal. There was a basketball court on the corner of Lexington Ave and Martine Ave. They had the lights on all night, and we would be out there playing basketball until 2 o'clock in the morning.

Baba: Oh, they were up on Battle Hill. Were they tall?

Rick: No, they're still around and always together all the time. I wish I could remember their names. I'll walk out of here and say, oh yeah. (Joe recalls these were probably the Livingston twins.)

Rick: Always seeing them together all the time. I wasn't at Winbrook a lot. Like I said, most of my people were all around the area, like the Rices, like Kenny Faulkner, but Winbrook was the core of the community.

Baba: Winbrook had its reputation for sure.

Rick: Yeah, most certainly.

Baba: So, what were the things that you did, where did you go for socializing, where did you go for a part-time job?

Rick: I used to work at Alexanders; I think that might have been my first job. I also had a job when there used to be an A&P in Greenburgh.

Baba: Where Staples is now?

Rick: No, no, right on route 119 (Tarrytown Road), and there was a little store there, and Sunday mornings I put together newspapers there as well.

Baba: So, you lived in Greenburgh proper?

Rick: I lived in Greenburgh right up behind where the Greenburgh Public Library is now, on that hill behind it where there used to be the Greenburgh Town Hall straight up the hill.

Baba: Ok yeah, because I lived on Washington Avenue. I came up with Donald Sledge and a few of those brothers that came out of Greenburgh -- The Corams, of course, were ever-present in Greenburgh.

Rick: Greenburgh was really like a small town; a few families would dominate the whole town, like the Mitchells.

Joe: You knew the Sudderth family?

Rick: Yeah, Sudderth family, it's a real family-centered place.

Baba: And Union Baptist was down the hill.

Rick: Union Baptist Church, yeah, when my Godmother, Tessa Edmondson, lived on Carlton Street; she was a member of Union Baptist and a nutritionist at the new Greenburgh Center.

Joe: There was a Martial Arts school in the Greenburgh Center and my brother, Sensei Mack, was friends with the Instructor, Clyde "Stickman" Coy.

Rick: I remember because I always heard about him --I didn't begin to do martial arts stuff until I got out of law school...

Baba: Where did you go to law school?

Rick: Brooklyn Law School.

Baba: That was good for you and has been good for you.

Rick: It's been alright, I'm not going to complain about it.

Baba: No use now.

Rick: No use now.

Rick: Practicing law for many years.

Baba: As I think about Greenburgh as a whole, I think about the Boy Scouts. Who was the scoutmaster, he had a daughter that sang? I can't think who, but we used to march in parades together. After the car accident in 1963, I was in Grasslands Hospital, and during that time, I was still in foster care. After I got out of the hospital, I moved to White Plains and got separated from that family, but there was a brand-new family for me here in White Plains. All those changes…

Rick: Something you said reminded me of growing up there. I had several parents, parents everywhere, I had parents when I went home, parents when I went out, parents when I went across town, it was a good thing. You don't have a life like that these days.

Baba: No, no, because of the makeup of communities and how they develop, that just doesn't happen anymore. Hopefully, someday in time, the cycle will come back around; the good thing is that we're still here and our memories are still here, and there are some places we can point to that existed when we were here. I think that is important of course. The people and the relationships you used to have are always paramount and community relationships. Do you think that any real community now still exists?

Rick: Yeah, I do.

Baba: As defined, how would you define community?

Rick: Yeah, that's how I found you, and that's why I'm here, but it's a digital community, so it's just moved to a different kind of place. It's not the same, but I watch things that you have to say, there are a lot of people that may not be physically here, you know, like in your location. You can't reach out and touch them or talk to them directly, but there's a community, a sort of digital community--I think the one that I had growing up was much better, but it's still better than having no connections.

Baba: Without the one that you had growing up, you couldn't have connected the memories. I would not have been there; I would have just been another foreigner on the screen. How do we correct that, and how do we use where we are now to stimulate a more significant influx of community, of family, of being together?

Rick: That's a fabulous question. I don't know how we could go about doing that --I don't know if such a thing would be possible.

Baba: Or needed?

Rick: May not be needed, absolutely.

Baba: I know in my lifetime if I didn't have friends and family, you know for me that's no life, in our fast-moving pace. If we must call ourselves "friends" on our little social media networks instrument... then let us be friends.

Rick: Exactly (laughter)...

Baba: Appreciate you coming brother, it's always good to connect with somebody who remembers the Societies.

Rick: You all were "Fly" brother, (laughter) Got your stuff together.

Baba: Then you remembered well...that part of my life was not in vain (laughter). Appreciate you, brother, stay strong and stay well, my brother.

Rick: Absolutely--You do the same.

CHAPTER 5

STORIES: KARATE AND OTHER MARTIAL ARTS - COMING OF AGE IN WHITE PLAINS

Karate and the self-defense schools we knew, a family tradition of martial arts-self-defense skills

Karate and The Self-Defense Schools We Knew:
By Joe Mack

When I came to White Plains, I knew of one major karate school on Main Street across from the Loew's Theatre. This school taught a Japanese style of karate called Kyokushin Kai. It was led by Sensi Shigeru Oyama, who many believe was a descendant of the legendary Master Mas Oyama and who had just arrived from Japan, but that was not the case. He was, however, handpicked by Mas Oyama to come to America to introduce the Kyokushin Kai style and open several schools, one of which was in White Plains.

The Winbrook Karate era stimulated a resurgence of Martial Arts in Westchester County.

The Egyptian Te/Sei Goju Karate System introduced "The Sleeping Death Kata," an advanced self-defense technique, and many others to White Plains and other Westchester County cities and towns, and a connection of martial arts with Manhattan, Brooklyn, the Bronx, and throughout New York City. The early architect of this style is described in the introduction of Sensei W. Mack to the Westchester region around the mid-'60s

Joe Mack Remembers:

During the latter part of the 1960s, a young Black belt who lived in Brooklyn moved to live with his family in White Plains and that Black belt was Sensei William Mack, who later became known as the Incredible Grandmaster Dr. Shihan W. Mack. Shihan Mack had honed his skills in the Dojos of Brooklyn, NY training with such great and renowned practitioners as Thomas LaPuppet, George Scofield, Moses Powell, and many others of that era. You may have guessed by now that Shihan Mack was my older brother, who then began his journey in White Plains by teaching students from all over the neighborhood, including many from Winbrook families who had little or no income to spare. Sensei taught many of these students for free and even encouraged them to bring some of their friends to his school. Sensei taught a style of Goju Ryu Karate that quickly became popular and drew students from throughout the community, including the Town of Greenburgh, NY.

Some of his early classes were taught in the basement of the projects but he later moved into his first Dojo across the street from 159 South Lexington Avenue in a building next to the laundromat. There Sensei Mack's legend continued to grow as he performed amazing feats of strength and martial arts displays. He was primarily known for bending steel bars around his neck, breaking boards, bricks, and cinder blocks seemingly with ease, during the many demonstrations that he performed throughout Westchester County over the years.

Sensei Mack was later invited to demonstrate at the esteemed "Oriental World of Self Defense" at Madison Square Garden, hosted by Grandmaster Aaron Banks. This was the first time the world got to see or read about a karate man attempting to break a 1000-pound block of solid ice with his head. News articles reported the karate master from Westchester, NY hit the ice so hard with his head that the sound echoed throughout the halls and chambers of the Garden's pavilion. Finally, after several attempts, the crowd roared as two large pieces of ice crashed to the floor, and Sensei Mack stepped back into his ready stance, letting out a "Kiai" sound so loud that it literally shook the rafters, to the amazement of everyone in attendance, and brought the crowd to their feet!

Never before had this feat been witnessed on American soil, and it left a vivid memory in the minds of all those who experienced the event. This helped to place

Sensei Mack at the top of the food chain and, as a result, he spent the better part of the next five years or so, fending off the challenges from karate experts from all over who wanted to exchange technique with him or see where they stood.

The list included greats like Sensei Earl Monroe, Grandmaster Alan Lee (reported to be the Uncle of Bruce Lee), Sensei Tommy May, Master Billy Richardson, and yes, even the elusive and mysterious Master from New York, Master Kareem Allah, to name a few. This also endeared Sensei Mack to Grandmaster Aaron Banks, who later personally inducted him into the New York Martial Arts Hall of Fame. It is around this time that Sensei Mack was promoted to Master and later Grandmaster in the arts and went on to develop his style known as Universal Goju Ryu Kai, which stands as one of the most profound martial arts schools in the city of White Plains to this day.

Grandmaster Shihan Mack - Ice Breaking Demonstration New York 1990

Over the years, in addition to his several sites in White Plains, Shihan Mack opened schools in Mamaroneck, Ossining, Peekskill, and Poughkeepsie, and several other places before establishing his main Dojo on Ferris Avenue in White Plains where it has now been located for several decades.

Grandmaster Shihan Mack has developed a litany of great students, many of whom either lived in Winbrook or had family members and friends who did. This list would include The Honorary Senior Master Sensei Marland Jefferies, Master Bahru Seward, Master Joe, Sensei Sundan Seward, Sensei Rahku Lynk, Sensei Rasheen Reed, Instructor Gwen, Instructor LaQuon, Mali, Instructor Bae Mitchell, Gamal "Doc" Mack, George Mitchell, Willie Hodge, Tommy Hodge, Frederick Hodge, and any number of other outstanding students not listed. Master Bahru later recalls the names of the Black belts from the original Dojo to be Mali Seward, Rasheen Reed, LaQuon Burrows, Lahuri Dorns, Ade Nash, Rahku Lynk, and himself.

Shihan also played a key role in the development of the legendary Kung Fu Grandmaster previously known as Sifu Tony Watts from White Plains, who has since relocated to New York City and opened several highly successful programs of his own. As well as early years training and development of Sensei Clyde "Stickman" Coy, who went on to become a legendary teacher of the Kyokushin Kai School of Karate in Greenburgh, NY. and Sensei Randall Ephraim, who now owns a successful Dojo in Tennessee and so many others.

Karate demonstration on Ferris Ave - Rahku Lynk and LaQuon Burrows - photo 1970s

As another author and highly regarded martial artist from Winbrook, Jason Rhodes, once put it. "For White Plains Martial Artist, it appears that all roads began or came through Sensei Mack."

The following excerpt, "Return to the 36 Chamber…...For Real!" is an article written by Jason Rhodes (Bldg. 135), who collaborated with my oldest son, Gamal "Doc" Mack (Bldg. 159), with contributions from Darrick Chatman, Randall Ephraim,

Stanya Balogun, and Monife Balogun. This passage is a summation of Jason's story and it details a true recollection of martial arts events in White Plains as witnessed by the eyes of the presenters.

"Return to the 36 Chamber......For Real!"

By Jason Rhodes

I sat with my back up against the bleachers. I surveyed all around me; red sashes, dragons, tigers, red, white, and black gi's. A wide plethora of Martial Arts practitioners seemed to be represented. There is no one style. There are simply several ways to "catch a beat down."

Up until that point, I had studied Kenpo Karate for ten years (I am approaching twenty years now). I was a second-degree Black belt. My lineage, traced backward, from my Instructor, Joe Palanzo to his Instructor, Ed Parker, Sr., to his Instructors; Chinese born; William K.S. Chow (Kung Fu/ Chinese Kempo of Kara Ho) and Japanese born; James Mitose (Kosho Ryu Kempo or Yoshida Ryu).

They reportedly learned from a long line of family members, respectively, tracing all the way back to the Shaolin Temple, Bodhidharma, and the soon-to-be warrior monks that he would train; centuries of skill passed down.

Kenpo itself is an eclectic art that is comprised of Boxing, Karate, Kung Fu, Jujitsu, and Judo.

None of that mattered at the moment. As the saying goes, "It's not the Art, but it's the practitioner that ensures victory!"

The setting was the Baltimore International Martial Arts Tournament. It is one of, if not "the", biggest Martial Arts Tournaments in Maryland.

I thought of myself in the moment, but I didn't stay there; that thought lent to others. I thought about Martial Artists, who became legends. I thought of the stories I heard over time, a few I witnessed. Stories that no one would believe, if not told; stories that didn't take place in a sanitized environment, with referees and stoppages, but in the merciless and unforgiving streets.

The 1970s

Once upon a time, a knock came at a steel Project door; 159. Another "Stranger"; Martial Artist, had appeared from out of town, to issue a challenge to Sensei Willie Mack (respectfully now; Shihan Willie Mack; Egyptian Te Goju/ Universal Goju). Sometimes these "strangers" came from various cities and states. They had all heard of Sensei Willie Mack, almost like a scene in the televised show the "Highlander," they too had a quest to become Immortal (at least in reputation); they sought to take his "Crown."

"There could be only One!"

The "Strangers" had heard of his "Legend" and had traveled far and wide to dethrone him. "Strangers" skilled in various Martial Arts, some of their Arts exotic.

Sensei Willie Mack sipped his beverage, calmly took another bite of his sandwich/meal, and followed this particular "Stranger" down the stairs of 159 to the playground.

Sometimes, Sensei Willie Mack, bored with the challenge before him, would allow his Black Belts/Shodans an opportunity to dispatch of the challenger, for they were an extension of him. Black, young, mostly bald-headed disciples, such as Bahru Seward, Rasheen Reed, Lahuri Dorns, Rahku Lynk, Laquon Burrows, Mali Seward (female), and Ade Balogun. They all had previously forged themselves in the fire; operating on the premise; iron sharpens iron. They were extremely dangerous and would not disappoint!

There were five belts in the Egyptian Te Goju system: White, Yellow, Blue, Brown, and Black. You would earn every Belt; nothing was free. You toiled and trained in the elements; hot, cold, freezing, in the woods, on concrete, and in sticky conditions; places like the old Carver Center on Lexington Avenue and the Blue House on Fisher Avenue, doing knuckle and fingertip push-ups along the way.

"Welcome to the 36 Chamber.........For Real"

Sensei Willie Mack would often challenge his own Brown and Black Belts.

"All of you vs. Me; I can only use my feet."

His legs extending, slicing into flesh, with the force of a sledgehammer. His stone hands lay idle to his side. His head, which he used to break casket-sized ice blocks and brick, also laid idle.

This is what makes a Legend!

Former student; Monife Balugon states:

"During each session, there were the three levels of teaching, Physical, Spiritual, and Mental. Sensei taught the value of hard and soft breathing for the body, the high level of mental focus to enable you to see through an object before landing the strike to break the object as well as the life lessons such as Family First, the importance of building and having your own businesses along with proper nutrition. Regardless of his choices in life, he instilled this way of life in his students."

Back to the playground, another "Challenger" defeated, they would pick up their teeth, hug their broken ribs, limp, back upstairs; defeated, where Sensei Willie Mack graciously fed them!

Shihan Willie Mack; never conquered!

For White Plains Martial Arts and Artist, it appears that all roads began or came through Sensei Mack.

A Ripple -E36 Chamber; White Plains Nighttime 1970s

Metro-North, two young brothers (in the cultural sense, not related) exit the train at the White Plains stop. They are coming from Manhattan, Chinatown. They've been training with a disciple of the fabled "Ip Man" (Bruce Lee's Teacher; see Ip Man movies starring Donnie Yen, also the fantastic biopic "The Grandmaster" starring Tony Leung Chiu-Wai")

The Disciple who taught the class was legendary Moy Yat (According to Inside Kung-Fu Magazine, he was "...considered among the greatest martial arts teachers of all time.")

Historically, many Asians were forbidden to share the Martial Arts with Foreigners; they were deemed to be giving away Chinese/Japanese secrets.

They felt that they were Martial Arts descendants of the founding Fathers; Martial Arts strategists, practitioners, Generals like those who formed China by merging the "Three Kingdoms" in 200 A.D.; predecessors like; Cao Cao of Wei, Liu Bei of Shu, and Sun Quan of Wu.

The Japanese pondered the great Samurai of the past; Miyamoto Musashi (undefeated author of "The Book of the Five Rings") Tokugawa Leyasu, Toyotomi Hideyoshi, Oda Nobunaga. The latter three would unify Japan after the Warring States Period (1467-1590). (See all about-japan.com, Japan's 12 Most Famous Samurai)

They (the brothers) have on their Black Kung Fu Gi's. They are training in Wing Chun. They exit the stairwell only to be greeted by challengers equally skilled and just as deadly!

The street lamps shine on the black pavement as fists, hand swords, joint locks, kicks, knees were exchanged in a fight for survival. This scenario repeated itself in various venues for a period of time.

The parallels are stunning; years prior, similar scenarios would play themselves out in the streets of Hong Kong with Ip Man himself and some of his disciples. For example, student; Wong Shun Leung has been noted to have personally won up to 60 bare-knuckle fights on the streets of Hong Kong.

In time, cooler heads would prevail, and the "Arts" shared, but only after near-death exchanges!

This was not Urban Legend; this is what actually happened on the streets of White Plains.

There has always been an interesting mix between "Urban America" and Martial Arts, think "Wu-Tang Clan", a strong movement primarily in the entertainment genre; but there have always been fearless "Brothers" "Living It" (see Forgotten Fury-YouTube)

"Elevation Nation" with its founder Randall Ephraim laid the first blueprint; mixing Black culture, Martial Arts, and music; In his own words:

Elevation Nation spearheaded, introduced, and controlled the B. Boy, or what is known now as the Hip Hop movement. We started out our crew as LuZu. LuZu was supposed to be a chapter of ZuLu Nation, a so-called upstate chapter back in 79. Africa Bambaata was expanding his gang of B. Boy's all over New York. From the biggest to the smallest towns. I was traveling back and forth from the Bronx and Mount Vernon in a time when if you weren't from those particular neighborhoods, you couldn't walk through these neighborhoods even in daylight! But at a young age, I always knew how to conduct myself in dangerous places, with my hands, and the gift of gab, so I was always comfortable in tough situations. My stepfather used to live on 174 and Longfellow, across the bridge from the Bronx River Project. At 14yrs of age, I made friends with a kid named; "Will Kid" Wilbur McCuller; R.I.P., first cousins to Amy Hopgood Bauman and Toni Tweedy from Lake St. and the Projects. Bear with me cause I'm trying to make this short. We were street kids doing our thing trying to express ourselves through a subculture that was foreign, frightening, and definitely not accepted in the central- northern part of Westchester County. So, it sat well with a place called the "Winbrook Projects". If you are over 40...forget that...till this day, it's the place where outsiders tell their children that it's forbidden land! ...lol. All of the so-called tough, and street innovators came there to either learn, test or practice their skills. So, when Lake St., Ferris, and DeKalb were still trying to push less threatening music, "DISCO"! We reintroduced the old spiritual beats of R&B and breaks going back-to-back, on two SL 210 Technic Turntables and a microphone, and people who were going through the same struggle related joined in and let us lead the way! If you want to understand what Elevation was all about, just think of how Wu-Tang projected in the '90s almost 20yrs after the fact. We had a top graffiti artist, Barry Johnson, "Country ", Security crew, Moe, Tyral Johnson, The twins Rondu and Kendu, Mays D.J.' Son of Sam, D.I., Grandmaster Boo. M.C.s Myself, Will Kid, Doc Dee, Bingo Rock, Crowd Control, Sifu, Ez Gee aka, "Griff" Rodney Griffin, just to name a few! They were key figures of what was going on in White Plains at that time. The only other crew in White Plains that compared to us at that time was Kevin Gore, who was a genius, R.I.P., and Pierre David Garcia Albert, who was respected heavily on our side of town from his family. He had a crew, the "Cosmic Brothers." And didn't make that total transformation of what is known as hip hop today. While they still played a lot of discos at the time. I have to give Gore and Pierre their props though! People came from all over to get with our small little click from White Plains. Back then, Cats like L.B. Wako 3, M.M. Big West came up after us. They benefited off of our hard street, gang banging, and street hustling so that they didn't necessarily have to do what we did to get their names out there. After our crew came, the above people mentioned, LB., DJ Chappelle,

Destro, Quick, to name a few. Shout out to the S.W.C. aka Baby Elevation, and a whole mess of Brothers and Sisters that I didn't mention in this scribe!

Randall Ephraim, aka; R.E., a practitioner himself of Kyokushin Karate, was also taught by Sensei Willie Mack, Clyde Coy, also known as "Stickman,", Professor Tony Watts, in addition to Moy Yat.

It should be noted that "Mas Oyama, was a karate master who founded Kyokushin Karate, considered the first and most influential style of full-contact karate". (see Wikipedia)

The 1980s

Eyewitness to the E36 Chamber; 1980s Strateman Park/Winbrook

It was a warm 80-degree summer day in Strateman Park; all of the normal activity was taking place, box ball, jump rope, card playing, laughing, dancing, cracking jokes, kids on swings, beautiful women, wooden puck hockey inside the shade house, music, ice cream, smoking, and drinking.

A serious game of Basketball was being played on the main court. The Big men were shoving, picking, yelling, and competing.

The teams were going back and forth, exchanging leads. A jump shot, fast break, nice pass, then layup.

Back and forth, back and forth...

The sideline was crowded, a mix of every age, kids to adults. There were adults who had "next," anxiously awaiting for the game to conclude. To "lose"; would mean; going back to the end of the line and waiting an hour or more to play again; the stakes were high!

Above our heads, on the fourth, second, seventh, and fifth floors, bodies hung out the windows of the respective buildings that were adjacent to the playground; 159 and 33. Individuals yelled down from their perch as if they had suite/box seats!

After he sunk the "bucket", Buster puffed his chest and declared, "Game!"

Sifu Watts held the ball tightly and stoically disagreed, he uttered, "Foul, respect the call!"

Buster simmered and slightly escalated the situation, "Naw, F$&@ that!"

Eight ballplayers, who had seen this "scene" before, recognized the changing mood and shifted as the budding confrontation ignited. They cleared the court like a Magician snatching a tablecloth, leaving the salt and pepper shakers unmoved; "Buster and Sifu."

Buster and Sifu remained at half court, locked into a "warrior thing."

Sifu, with the ball, tucked under his right arm. Buster "jawing", nose to nose; explicit flying; they stood in the middle of the circle under the bright sunshine as if they were two Lions refusing to retreat.

Sifu, in top shape, had the physical appearance of a superhero, Buster more of a wide-bodied villain.

I immediately saw it through my own prism.

"Buster, the Gangsta. Vs. Sifu Watts, the Martial Arts Master"

I read a lot of comics, and that's how my mind chose to relate, it made it more palpable.

I could see the dark ink and shadows as if it were a photo still, etched on the cover of a graphic novel.

"Animosity, Animosity," Sifu calmly spoke.

Words I had never heard!

"Animosity Man, Animosity!"

We (kids) turned to one another and mocked to one another, like a strange Greek Chorus:

"Animosity Man, Animosity!"

We laughed because we didn't know what else to do, as Buster and Sifu stood nose to nose.

Sifu parted his arms, and the ball released, bounced, and rolled away.

Sifu stood with two massive wings to his side, Buster less than a foot from him. Sifu brought his right hand up with lightning speed and seemingly waved in the direction of Buster's left eye returning his powerful wing to his right side as if he were holstering a six-shooter to his waist!

A curdling scream came from Buster's wide-open mouth; his eyeball; lay on his cheek, with a bloody exposed optic nerve attached like a branch holding an apple.

He tried to shove it back in, screaming; his shrill, piercing the frivolity of the playground; he took off, running to the hospital!

Sifu walked off the court to cheers of "Animosity Man, Animosity" (at least from us little kids) just as cool as Bruce Lee did when he defeated O'Hare in "Enter the Dragon".

Sifu Watts' early beginnings include being taught by Shihan Willie Mack, Moy Yat, and he would later study under Moses Powell, Sanuces Ryu Jujutsu system. Grandmaster Tony D. Watts is the owner of the Wing Chun Ju-jutsu Ryu Kung Fu.

The 2000s

I check my gloves and they feel funny; maybe it's the wrap underneath. I don't have time for that now. To the right of me, I watch two practitioners engage in "point sparring". (Think "Danielson" vs. Cobra Kai at The Karate Kid Tournament) They bounce, circling one another. The taller opponent sees his opportunity and launches into a spinning back kick; his heel comes crashing down on the temple of his well-built opponent. His opponents' body instantly goes limp and collapses like a redwood tree in the forest, bouncing off the floor.

The mid-1970s

Sifu Kevin Martin shoots a straight flat pointed hand at a tree. Pieces of bark splinter, he rakes down, clawing smaller pieces of bark. He is sharpening his tool. His hand becomes a knife. Over time, the roundness of his fingertips flattens to the equivalent of a blade.

On another day, he proceeds to strike a brick, dislodging it from the Projects facade.

And on yet another day, he walks through the snow on bare feet. Moving through Winbrook in a Black Kung Fu Gi and Chinese Japs on his feet. This stands as a heavy contrast to the Black fashions of the day.

He too has answered the knocks at his door (11 Fisher), confrontations in the hallway; shifting his opponent's nose from God-given center; to the newly right, with a vicious roundhouse kick.

He would go on from Winbrook to Special Police Forces with the United States Air Force, guarding President Reagan and Imelda Marcos due to his Martial Arts prowess. He was invited to demonstrate Wing Chun at the Legendary Shaolin Temple, the first Black Man to do so.

Sifu Kevin Martin was also trained by Shihan Willie Mack, as well as Moy Yat.

2019- January

CNN headlines read, "Cops say a would-be kidnapper chased a woman -- into a karate studio. That was a bad move."

In fact, it was a bad move; Kyokoshun Instructor, Randall Ephraim confronted the would-be attacker and introduced him to years of Martial Arts training. The big man left horizontal and on a stretcher.

Need I say it, this is strength personified. "Man"; through discipline, dedication, and commitment achieving new heights, leaving the sphere of ordinary to extraordinary; Excellence achieved. It's "Ali" in bellicose rhetoric; "Float like a butterfly, sting like a bee"; realized, through ancient principles and application.

Winbrook is reaching and pulling in from across the World, as well as outputting, by, influencing, protecting, demonstrating, teaching, and defending.

They are who we draw strength from, point to as evidence; "It can be done." It is the story that should be told.

PostScript.

To be clear, Martial Arts has always had a Black influence, if not beginning. The oldest Martial Art might be the Nubian Martial Art of Wrestling.

Fellow Martial Artist Jonathan Bynoe States;

"Other systems of combat were Kuta translated as defender of the Pharaoh. It's an unarmed and armed combat system practiced by the bodyguards of the Pharaohs. The stick fighting art out of Kemet is called Tahteeb, and it is the influential stick fighting system to many African stick fighting arts such as Zulu Impi and Kali/Arnis/Escrima of the Philippines." (See "Origins of Martial Arts: The Real History" by Jonathan Bynoe)

By Jason Rhodes

Contributors; Darrick Chatman; Gamal Mack; Randall Ephraim; Stanya Balogun; and Monife Balogun

A special thanks to those above for sharing their stories and guiding me towards accuracy and truth.

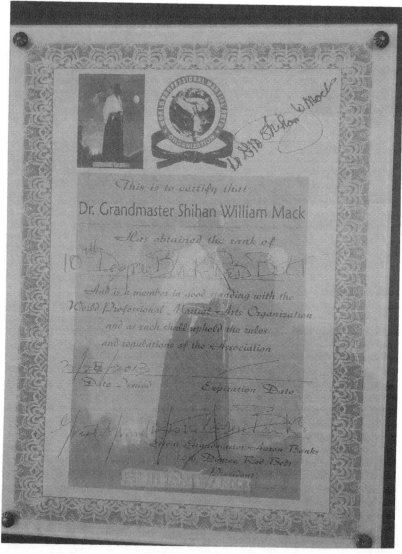

Dr. Grandmaster Shihan Mack's Promotion to 10th Degree Black Belt, **2013**

Joe's Story:

Sensei Mack's younger brother, Joe, was better known around the area for his boxing skills, but it should be noted that he was also inspired by his brother's success in karate and decided to take a turn in studying the Martial Arts himself. Joe first engaged in some training with his brother to get his foundation in the Arts but later found himself practicing an Okinawan Shorin Ryu Style, Matsubayashi Ryu, with Sensei Zenko Heshiki in a Dojo in Manhattan, NY.

This Dojo was located not far from Joe's job in the city, and he stopped there to train when he got off work each evening while waiting for the traffic at Grand Central Station to calm down a bit. His journey through the Arts ultimately led to Joe becoming a self-defense instructor while in the military service, studying Tae Kwon Do under Master Pak in Norfolk, VA, and obtaining a Shodan Black Belt Degree in Black Hawk Hapkido. Joe later received 5th Degree Black Belt honors in his brother's school in White Plains, The Universal Goju Ryu Kai School of Karate.

Even during the time Joe spent away from home in the military service, he never failed to come back to White Plains to visit his mother and son, Gamal, in 159, and his brother's karate school, which was being held in the new Carver Center -The Blue House - up on Fisher Avenue at the time. It was during one of these visits that Joe brought one of his closest friends up to the projects to hang out for the weekend. Joe and E.C. Shingles had met while in Marine Corps Boot Camp and out of the will to survive their grueling training, banded together and became friends for life.

E. C. lived in Harlem and welcomed the chance for a change of pace up in White Plains. E. C. was also a karate practitioner who held a 3rd Kyu Brown Belt in the style of Shotokan Karate. Joe told E. C. they would head up to White Plains and to bring his Gi so they could visit Sensi's Dojo for a workout. During this time many of Sensi's students were fairly new, ranging from White Belt through the 6th Kyu Green Belt level.

On the way, Joe picked up another 5th Kyu Japanese style, Kyokushin Kai, a student he knew from Mt. Vernon named Taboo, and they all headed to his brother's Dojo. After a brisk period of training, it was time for what's called freestyle sparring-kumite, where students got to test out their skills and technique with another student, exchanging technique.

Sensei walked around the room and told his highest Kyu student, Bahru Seward, to step forward. He then told Joe's friend, E. C., to step forward. Joe had seen Bahru in action and knew he was no joke, but he'd also seen E. C. hit a Navy Corpsman with a front kick so powerful it made him fold up like a napkin!

It was a closely fought match and ended with both parties coming away with a measure of respect for each other's skills. Sensei enjoyed joking around with his brother, so he then told Taboo to step forward and called out Joe for the next session. Unfortunately, Joe landed a driving front kick to the midsection, and the match ended early, as Joe was quick to check and make sure Taboo was ok. That was the way of karate in White Plains in those days, on any given day and in any given school you could end up in a tough sparring session, woe upon he who was ill-prepared when that day came!

Another karate story that Joe often told to a close friend from the Navy named Art Moran. It describes the day Sensei took Joe, Black belt, and State Trooper Thurman, students George Mitchell and Stuart Dotson down to the Bronx for an early morning sparring session at Sensei Billy Richardson's Goju School of Karate.

After training was done, each student lined up next to the wall and was called out for sparring by the teacher, saying, "How do you speak...Green Belt, Brown Belt, or Black Belt?" Soon two belts of equal power would be on the floor in battle. Sensei Richard went all around the room, and most of the matches ended in either a knockout or a student saying, "I cannot continue Sensei." Finally, he got to Joe, Sensei Mack's brother, who had put his gi and his belt away for the day with no intentions of sparring. When Sensei Richardson said, "How do you speak" Joe replied, "I cannot speak today, Sensei." Sensei Richardson then told all of the students to have a seat and said, "You shall now see two Masters' at work."

Sensei Mack was called to the floor, to which he obliged, and Sensei Richardson stepped front as well. They respectfully bowed to each other, and there were several tense moments before the two experts collided in a flurry of kicks and punches, so fast that the human eye could only hope to follow.

When they jumped back, both men were panting, but both gis were hardly ruffled. Again, they collided; this time, something extraordinary occurred. There was a loud thud! All of a sudden the action stopped, seemingly in mid-combat, and Sensei Richardson stood straight up, called the school to the floor, and dismissed the class.

The head black belts then turned and walked into the locker with Sensei Richardson leading the way followed by Sensei Mack, the two most senior men in the Dojo. It was later revealed that the loud thud came from Sensei Richardson getting hit by a reverse heel kick in the ribs from Sensei Mack that would have literally paralyzed the average human! However, Sensei Richardson summoned up the strength to "Ibuki" breathe deep, so as not to show pain and was still able to dismiss his class. However, upon entering the locker room, he collapsed, and Sensei Mack had to lift him up to the bench and give him some water. The spirit of a true Master is that none of this occurred in the presence of his students and neither of these Brothers in the Martial Arts reveled in the defeat of the other.

CHAPTER 6

MORE STORIES: TRACK & FIELD, BASKETBALL AND BOXING – NOTABLE HIGHLIGHTS

Stories and Experiences:

This is what we found out, talked about, reflected upon, recalled - related to those we knew and the spirits of those no longer with us…

Joe Recalls Track Events:

Sports were big in White Plains, and Winbrook had its share of talented athletes. During that era, track & field was dominant at the high school and boasted such dynamic athletes as Otis Hill, Larry James, Carl Reed, David Jackson, Cedric Thomas, Herb, and Ronnie Moss, and the Mosley brothers among many others; all skillfully trained to perfection by Coach Kehe from White Plains High. The sprint relay teams were particularly impressive, and Coach Kehe often relied on Carl Reed, Otis Hill, Dave Jackson, and Larry James to bring home the victory with Cedric Thomas as the primary alternate in case any one of them couldn't go.

This outstanding collection of track talent, White Plains High School's reputation, and several other factors led to several trips to the prestigious Penn Relays for the track team and, one of those trips provided lasting memories for all of us to share. The year was 1966, and the event was the 4 X 440 relay. White Plains had already run some impressive times in this event, and there was no doubt they would be in contention among some of the best high school teams in the country, but few were prepared for what was about to occur at that year's track festival.

It was a rainy day, and the old cinder track at Franklin Field, in need of repair, was covered with mud when the race began. The gun sounded and a group of the fastest high school track teams in the country that year took off, with White Plains High getting in the mix early. However, as the race progressed, the field tightened, and it became evident there would be a battle for the lead after each baton exchange.

Coming home after the final exchange, White Plains had just begun to extend their lead when Otis Hill took the baton and quickly left no doubt he was "in it to win it!" After about 200 meters, Otis kicked into a gear that few had ever witnessed, not even some of his own teammates! The crowd went wild, being led in their cheers by several White Plains students, Jamal Koram and Glenn Rogers, along with other friends and family members who had traveled with them to provide encouragement and support.

The now-famous "Whooop...Whooop!" sound made when someone is either pulling away from the field or being caught from behind by the field started slowly and rose to a crescendo as the anchor leg blasted down the home stretch. When all was said and done, Otis crossed the line approximately 20 yards in front of the pack with a time of 3 minutes, 17.9 secs just .04 sec off the meet record! It was truly an amazing day.

Adding icing to the cake, White Plains High also won the Two-Mile Relay that day! When four 880 runners, Leonard Hadley, Thomas Jordan, Raymond Jordan, and Darryl Turner, combined to run on this distance relay team and won their event in an impressive time of 7:59.2 sec. to claim victory over another stacked field of runners. Man, oh man, White Plains was putting on a show on one of the biggest stages for track and field in the nation...if not the entire world!

That same year, following their dominant performance at the Penn Relays, the 4 X 220 relay team of Carl Reed, Larry James, David Jackson, and Otis Hill lined up again in an invitational meet at St. John's University to take on some of the best teams in the state. They crossed the finish line in a winning time of 1:25.4 seconds, setting a new National High School record for that event! A week later the same group was invited back to St. John's University for another invitational but this time to participate in the 4 x 440 relay. The race was spectacular, and the results were the same, another victory and another National High School record time of 3:12.7!

These five members of the relay team; Larry James, Otis Hill, David Jackson,

Carl Reed, and alternate Cedric Thomas kept in touch and remained friends long after their high school years. Larry went on to attend Villanova and became a standout runner on the college level for which he earned the nickname "The Mighty Burner." Larry also participated in the 1968 Summer Olympic Games, winning a gold medal as a member of the 4 X 400-meter relay team and a silver medal behind Lee Evans world record time in the open 400 Meter event, with both Larry James and Lee Evans breaking the previous world record.

Only two members from that era are alive today, Coach Kehe and David Jackson, but they lived to see the group be inducted to The Penn Relays Wall of Fame (2016) and The White Plains High School Hall of Fame (2016) to be enshrined and remembered forever. They will always live on in our hearts and memories, bringing pride to Winbrook and White Plains High whenever and wherever we go.

Baba Jamal Remembers Larry James:

Larry James: Talk about silence! Larry was a quiet brother. He was very friendly, and everyone respected him. If during that time, we had to select who would eventually go to the Olympics, it is plausible that no one would have selected Larry James. Only those who had watched him grow and who knew his tenacity would have even included him in an International Olympics Games competition. But there he was on T.V., and he was in the mix of that "fist in the air" controversy of the "68" Games and what led up to it. But through it all, Larry remained steadfast, true to what he came there for, and represented those who knew him well. He was truly a winner, a leader, and a friend. R.I.P. Larry James.

Joe Mack remembers Otis Hill, off-track:

We wondered why we would always see him at the projects, being from Ferris Avenue and all. This was due to a fine sister named Sandra, but we're not going to butt into other people's business… In the projects, Joe Mack reminds us; we did look out for each other in those days.

Baba Jamal on Otis Hill and Others

OH! One more thing, as far as football was concerned, we knew that when Otis got the football, there would be yards gained. And we can't forget Charlie Sassar (Was he from Ferris Ave?). Charlie Sassar attended college at Florida A & M University, along with Otis Hill and Butch Mabry.

What wonderful memories. Particularly of high school, and those "crooning" times in front of 159 with Joe Mack, Charlie Sassar, Big Joe Day, Irving Robinson, Dennis Silas, Downy Flakes, and others, including James Coram, whose Sister, Joyce Coram was a well-known high school singer. Anyway, Looney, as he was called, could sing too. George Young could hold that baritone. That's partly how the hometown group, "The Societies," were born, with Darryl Cole, James Coram, George Young, Chuckie Addison, basically from Winbrook, and later joined by Bobby Jackson from Greenburgh.

"Under the Boardwalk"

From the high school halls to the champion music group of Westchester County! Winbrook was represented well! You remember seeing us on the Float at the Thanksgiving Day Parade as we rode up Main Street, on the "Show Mobile" crooning, and waving. And when we made that turn from Main Street, on to Mamaroneck Avenue, at the corner of RKO and Macy's…. Darryl Cole, George Young, Bobby Jackson, Kenneth "Chuckie" Addison, and James "Looney" Coram were the singers…the Band was Reggie Life and Louis Archer.

I can remember seeing my sister Sharon, and my nephew in the crowd, and folks from Winbrook waving as we made the turn and stopped for a minute in the bleachers we sang!! 135, 33, 159, Wyanoke Street and Greenburgh/Parkway Gardens in the HOUSE!

Joe Mack Recalling Larry James:

Larry James: You can't think of Otis Hill without thinking of Larry James. The "Mighty Burner," as he was dubbed by Sports Illustrated after a splendid performance at the Penn Relays one year. Larry was an Olympic champion in the mile relay and a silver medalist in the 400 meters at the 1968 games.

He was most noted, however, as a "Class Act" in every part of his life. He was highly respected by his fellow Olympic teammates and was considered the "voice of reason" during the Black Power movement at the 1968 Olympic Games in Mexico City, which resulted in two members of the team being stripped of their medals and ejected from the village.

Larry left me with two very profound memories; one was when he came home from the Olympic Games and spoke at the Carver Center to all the younger brothers and sisters who were still in high school. I was sitting somewhere near the front when he took out this huge Gold Medal, the biggest thing I'd ever seen, passed it around to let us know how we could achieve anything we wanted in life if we were willing to work hard enough for it. I knew then I wanted to dedicate myself to running like he had done, and this was when I first decided to make the sacrifice of hard, intense training in track and field. My track career was cut short in high school due to having surgery and not being able to run my senior year, but the memory of Larry talking to us that night never left me and I went on to compete in the Navy during my military career. I also competed in Masters Track and Field, where I later became a State and National sprint champion...Thank you Larry for your inspiration and encouragement. RIP my brother.

The next memory was when Larry James came to visit me at Westchester Community College after I had been elected President of the Afro-American Society on campus. I was sitting in the office alone pondering my next move with the administration when Larry walked in. He had gone out of his way to find me and share some insight and guidance on how I could face the challenges ahead, and I never forgot that gesture on his part. We kept in touch and talked from time to time over the years, and the last time we spoke was about track and field, which his life centered around, and which had also become a big part of my life by that time as well.

Baba Jamal Reflections:

Track Excellence - White Plains in the Limelight.

Otis Hill (Ferris Avenue) …When you think about Otis, you think about speed and power. On the football field or the track team, and even on the dance floor! Lol.

The Brother could RUN! He teamed up with Charlie Sassar, Carl Reed (33 Winbrook), Larry James, and David Jackson (also from Winbrook). Otis was from Ferris Avenue and Larry James was from over by Fisher Avenue, behind the playground.

Otis Hill, Davie Jackson, and Charlie Sassar all played WPHS football as well.

There was so much talent in those five buildings but some of it never got beyond the five buildings and the parking lot.

And you can't think about Larry James, Carl Reed, Otis Hill, and Charlie Sasser without thinking about the relays! Back to Otis. If you thought you only saw him on the track, then you missed him on the "gridiron." Smoother than rumbling thunder, faster than lightning. By the time you figured out where he was, at the Saturday races, at Penn Relays, folks done left church, eating chicken for Sunday night supper, and you still wondering, scratching your head. Some of y'all so slow, you're probably still at the stadium in 2020, wondering when the game is gonna start? …

Those brothers tore it up in Philadelphia at the Penn Relays. I was there. Glenn Rogers' immediate family, friends of the family, and his relatives from New Jersey, and did I miss someone? I was just glad to be in that number with some close ones and such. Aunt Margie loved me. And Otis Hill - We all respect his Legacy, all these decades later.

But that was just one event. The track team was tearing up records during that time. But we know there are fast brothers and sisters wherever you go. I had a cousin from my birthplace, Greenburgh, NY., Carol A. Coram who was also making track records, and as dedicated to the sport as she has always been, she is probably out running while this is being written. Faster than I could say how fast she is!

But back to the White Plains track team, with which Winbrook was represented at just about every event, at the junior high and high school levels.

There was a well-known rivalry in New York State during the Otis Hill era between Julio Meade from Andrew Jackson High School in Queens, NY, and Otis Hill from Ferris Avenue, and White Plains High School. They met several times in 1966, running that 300 race. They ran the fastest times in the United States, and there was to be a showdown in the 300 at a competition in California.

The White Plains High School track team under Coach Dean Locks and Coach Kehe brought recognition to the entire city and Larry James was one of the few who got out of it with some notoriety and fame beyond high school and college, having run and won a gold medal in the Worldwide International Olympics. To this day, we are proud of all of them, of their accomplishments, and proud to have known and know all of them personally.

At the time we were putting this memoir together, Joe Mack recalled that he knew that Otis was a standout football player and how sometimes Joe would see him visiting one of the beautiful sister classmates, who lived in Joe's building, 159. He remembered: "We always respected one another." The last time I saw Otis, he was a schoolteacher living in Ossining, NY. He was one of those brothers you miss. Oh, and another football star was Charlie Sanders, who, after high school, played football at Florida A & M. University.

Which brings back a memory of when we were all at White Plains High at the same time, during our sophomore year in '65. Every day at lunchtime, we would gather and sing. I remember that happening in one of White Plains High School's buildings; while another singing group thing was happening across campus in another of the five buildings, on the other side of the WPHS campus (there were five buildings) …In fact, it was stimulation for Darryl Cole (135) and myself, from Wyanoke St., to start a singing group called the Societies. But that's a story, all by itself.

Yes, there was a lot of singing going on during lunchtime, at White Plains High, in the late 1960s, with other Winbrook inhabitants, friends, and such.

Baba Jamal Reflects:

Larry James and I always connected. His sister was in my '68 graduating class and his mother was always active in the community and knew my family (Corams) well.

We were related in an around the corner kind of way; you know, a cousin of a cousin who married a cousin who really wasn't a cousin but is now. How in one generation, there was a family falling out, or a kinship discovery, or any small matter. Sometimes it didn't take much to happen, and related folks didn't talk to each other anymore. Then, by "grace," along came a distant cousin who patched things up… well, sort of …who could tell the difference? lol

There was some kind of relationship between Larry and me. You know, how someone in his family may have been childhood friends or hanging out/churchgoing or a close friend of a cousin friend? Whatever it was, it has stuck and stayed. My sister, Sharon, represented our clan at Larry James' homegoing service. She was represented by our Greenburgh family and friends during her homegoing a couple of years later. Including Mama James (Larry's mother). Thank God for those who have shared time and space but are now physically gone. Praise God, for those who are now gone…and for those who are still here…and for grand and great-grandchildren on their way here. Amen. Ashe'

Baba Jamal:

Back to track…I remember that year of WPHS track glory. Aunt Margie Rogers, her son Glenn, maybe Bonnie, Deborah, and Wayne their crew, and some cousins from New Jersey. Aunt Evie Parker and her husband, Uncle Mel, Jan, Dean, and Judy, their children, James Coram, and others. We all went to the Penn Relays in Philadelphia, Pennsylvania, to see White Plains High School Track Team compete at the world-famous "Penn Relays."

What a good time that was! That was the year Larry James ran a phenomenal leg in the 4 x 4 Relay, when he "made up some distance, covering ground to make up some lost time, which I think it was. And we watched Raymond (Frog) Jordan and his brother(s) run that year. I believe they had another brother on the track team, as well. I believe their older brother was also on the track team. This reminds me of another set of brothers, Earl and George Rainey who lived in 225.

They ran track in the early sixties, setting the way for Otis Hill, and Carl Reed, Larry, Charlie Sasser, and others. It seems like I remember a track meet at the new White Plains High Track. I remember seeing my red-headed Brother, Chuckie Addison, coming around that first turn, ahead of the crowd!

Joe Mack Reflects:

I can remember the story often told by Baba Jamal of his days of playing basketball in White Plains and how he became a key player on the high school basketball team. He first points out that because of the severe injuries he suffered due to being hit by a car when he was a child, he was left with a limp for the rest of his life. He didn't let this stop him from achieving the things he desired, like performing in a singing group "The Societies" and dancing all over the stage or playing the game he loved…basketball!

Even though his limp was quite noticeable and, no doubt restricted some of his movements, Baba Jamal (then James Coram) would often come out on the courts at Winbrook and play pickup games with players like Cliff Livingston, Johnny Randolph, Herb, and Ronnie Moss, Eric Rhodes, myself, and any other players that happen to be there that day. Not only did Jamal hold his own, but he also excelled in many of these matchups with his smooth moves and jumpers from the elbow, along with slick moves to the basket that sometimes ended in explosive dunks!

Despite his ability to overcome his injuries and develop into quite an impressive ballplayer, Jamal says he tried out for the high school team every year and got cut every year. His feeling was that although the coaches saw the ability, he displayed during tryouts, they just couldn't get over the fact that he had that limp and couldn't bring themselves to keep him or give him a chance to play.

After a while, Jamal was content just to spend his time playing with the New York Poles and the JABO Rims from his neighborhood in Winbrook. Many of his friends on the high school team played with him on these teams as well, and he enjoyed the game just as much playing with them after school and during the summers.

Finally, before he graduated, Jamal was given a chance and made the team. The rest is history but suffice it to say that James went on to play basketball in college and even played some semi-pro basketball before retiring his sneakers to become Baba Jamal Koram, "The StoryMan," an African American Storyteller of high esteem. Lesson learned… all is not lost that seems lost. In times of despair, just keep pressing forward, it's not where you start but how you end that matters the most.

During those days, Black high school coaches were somewhat scarce and White Plains High School basketball team was noticed as a force to be reckoned with after being able to achieve a measurable amount of success. It was not lost on members in our community that Black coaches had to prove themselves many times over, and some believed that Coach Jeff was pressured not to play too many of his Black players at once, but there was never any concrete evidence of that fact. If there was any indication that he adhered to such demand, it never surfaced. It's just one of those things that will go down as an untold story in the annals of his team's history.

Boxing at The Cage Recreation Gym:

By Joe Mack

Many great fighters came out of the Cage boxing program and trained under the watchful eye of Coach Charlie Caserta. Some names that come to mind are Cleo Daniels, Herschel Jacobs, Willie Hodge, and Kenny Mack Sr. Later that same gym trained such top contenders as Carl "The Truth "Williams, Lou Savarese, Renaldo Snipes and, Buster Mathis. I believe legendary Heavyweight Champion Larry Holmes even spent some time working out at the Cage during his heyday.

Winbrook housing, compassionately referred to as "The Projects" also shared in the Cage boxing talent and one of the greatest Golden Gloves Champions to ever come out of that era was a lightweight named Kenny Mack Sr., who lived at 159 South Lexington Avenue. I was first introduced to the Cage as a youngster of about 12 or 13 years old. When I walked in one day and said, I wanted to box. Coach Caserta took one look at me, a tall skinny kid, and said, "Come with me." I followed him and he put me on a heavy bag in a dark corner of the gym and left me there for about a week without even looking in my direction. He said, "All I want you to work on is this jab!"

None of the other boxers in the gym paid me any attention either until near the end of the week when the chain holding the heavy bag to the ceiling snapped during one of my sessions and the bag came crashing to the floor! Everybody in the gym stopped dead in their tracks and Coach Caserta said, "Come on over kid, I think you're ready to spar." I learned the fundamentals of the trade in boxing and developed a pretty good jab before losing interest as a teenager and moving on to other things.

We lived on Ridge Street at the time, but a few years later we moved into Winbrook, 159, and I picked up the sport of boxing again. I went back to the Cage and told Coach Caserta I was more serious this time, and now I wanted to fight in the upcoming New York Golden Gloves competition. I was a tad bit bigger, a lot faster and a little tougher than before, so Coach told me to "Lace-em up and let's see what you've got, kid."

It was during this era that I met Kenny Mack, Sr. He also lived in Winbrook in the same apartment complex as me, and we had the same last name, but we were not related as far as either one of us knew. Kenny, by this time, had already become a well-known and established boxer from the Cage, having won a Golden Gloves Championship in his weight class several years earlier. When someone told him about me, Kenny came up to my apartment one evening and asked if I wanted to do road work with him the next day before going to the gym.

Road work is the early morning runs that boxers do to help with their conditioning and is a must for anybody who wants to seriously take up the sport. Kenny and I met about 4:30 or 5:00 AM that next morning and the rest is history. We became the best of friends, and I developed into a much better and more conditioned fighter. In that regard, I can say that Kenny Mack, Sr. was indeed my boxing mentor and a dear friend.

I can remember that Kenny had a sparring partner in the gym; I believe his name was Rocco, and man oh man, they could light up the ring with matches that looked like a war every round with every blow designed to end the fight! Kenny and Rocco would go blow for blow with amazing speed each round until the bell rang and then come back again for some more. Whenever they fought, all the other boxers training that day would stop and watch!

One day Kenny couldn't make it to practice, and Coach Caserta looked around the gym and said, "Little Mack, come on over here. I want you to give Rocco some work. He's got a big fight coming up next month and I need to make sure he's sharp!" My heart skipped a beat because I had seen the vicious battles between him and Kenny and knew I'd have my work cut out for me, but I figured if Coach had the confidence in me to make the call, I had to step up.

Now both Rocco and Kenny were a little lighter than me but with much more experience than I had at the time, along with the blinding speed that made their matches so much fun to watch. On the other hand, I was a few inches taller with deceptive punching power and, to the surprise of many, was nearly able to match Rocco in hand speed as well.

When the match started, Rocco charged across the ring and opened up with a blistering attack of body shots designed to put me away early. I side-stepped and returned a combination to the head with such speed and accuracy that it got his attention and made him realize it was going to be a long day. We then met in the middle of the ring and went toe to toe with head and body combinations bouncing off each other like a hailstorm on a bad night!

I dropped a hard right to the body just before the end of the round and saw Rocco stagger a bit to catch his balance. When the bell rang, I went back to my corner and waited for the next round but noticed Coach Caserta closing it out and telling Rocco that was enough work for the day. I went back to working on the heavy bag and only found out later that Coach Caserta knew Rocco had a big fight coming up and didn't think it was a good idea to leave him in the ring with me too long after seeing the first round.

The next day when Kenny Mack returned, he ran over and hugged me and said, "Man, I heard about your match with Rocco yesterday and everybody said it was quite a battle. They said you held your own with him and looked like you were ready to go again!" Kenny never knew how good it made me feel and how proud I was to hear that coming from someone like him, a legend in the ring and the person I most wanted to show I had what it takes to make it in the fight game. My boxing career was cut short due to an eye injury later that year during a boxing show match-up in Montrose, NY, but our friendship endured for many years thereafter.

Other fighters reported to have trained or worked out at The Cage over the following years included Maurice Sposato, Kid Sharky, Buster Mathis, Larry Holmes, Joe Torres, Jeff Miller, Bill Cook, Jimmy Williams, Carl "The Truth" Williams, Renaldo Snipes, Herschel Jacobs, and Big Cleo Daniels.

Baba Jamal Recalls:

The "Cage" was a training center for boxers, some martial arts, and more. It was located just off Main Street in White Plains. Herschel Jacobs and Cleo Daniels were the older pros, Kenny Mack and Joe Mack (no relation, but they both lived in 159), Sensei Willie Mack, a world-renowned Martial Artist, and Joe Mack are brothers from the same mother, Ms. Mary Mack, whose grandson is Gamal Mack. Buster Douglas, Eugene Battle, and Lorenzo Battle are Baba Jamal's brothers from another mother. "Whew!" And that's just a piece of the story!

CHAPTER 7

THE JABO RIMS - BASKETBALL EVENTS TO REMEMBER

Joint Action for Black Organization (JABO) was a community group formed by Joe Mack, Baba Jamal, and a few others in the late '60s primarily to look out for the needs of the Black folks in Winbrook and throughout our neighborhood.

Joe Mack and James Coram realized that while JABO was an effective organization, not many of the younger brothers in the area were getting involved. They then devised a plan to create the "JABO Rims," a summer league basketball team that would go on to play a number of games in and around the city throughout the summer.

We were all out of high school at the time, but The Rims were comprised of some of the best high school players of our day. Along with James Coram and Joe Mack, people like Eric Rhodes, Johnny Randolph, Cliff Livingston, Bill Cain, Marvin Lewis, Ernest Saunders, Kenny Cain, Morris "Cowboy" Green, Freeman Beville, Steve Washington, Ernest Dimbo, Don McLaughlin, and others came together to create a formable squad that wasn't easy to beat. What evolved from there was a series of games played in the various playground neighborhoods in White Plains, with a few even extending out into the city.

Challenges were made and answered in battles against Lake Street teams from the Valley, with one Sunday afternoon game ending in a fight between Frog Jordan and Marvin Lewis. We won the game, and the issue on the court was resolved after a few blows so, all's well that ends well.

Baba Jamal Remembers Marvin Lewis:

Marvin Lewis – He was big and tall in high school and later grew into a man among men who I would guess was about 6' 10", and close to three hundred pounds. Despite his size, he had a gentle heart and always seemed to care about others. It was that same heart that would develop problems and later which took his life at an early age. He was well-liked by all who knew him, but because of his size and demeanor, he became a target for some of the hardheads, who wanted to establish a reputation at Marvin's expense. He was a good friend and a good brother. One incident that hangs in our hearts and minds is when the newly formed "JABO Rims" basketball team was playing on the outdoor court at the Eastview School in the Valley. It was a "Winbrook versus The Valley" contest. It must have been a sight: Big Marvin, Limping Looney aka James, Slim Joe Mack, Smooth Eric Rhodes, Jump Shot Cliff Livingston, etc. Well, long story short, after some pushing and elbowing by Frog against Marvin. It got into a fistfight, and Marvin was not a fighter. Joe Mack stepped in and had a few words with Frog, (and I thought I had a "nickname!"). Most of us had a reputation of sorts that some folks didn't want to test. And others were waiting for a chance to take away somebody else's reputation. It was like that on that day, on that lopsided court. The Valley had some power, now; but when you thought about Winbrook, and then about where Joe trained, and if that wasn't enough; you thought about who his brother was, even though he never relied on that, nor was there ever a time that his relationship with Sensei Mack was ever mentioned; it was still known, yet rarely mentioned in any type of circumstance… and then if you looked at the members of the JABO Rims Basketball Team and thought about their relatives and just as important was who they were on their own terms. There were a few things to consider before confronting certain brothers. Fortunately, and I don't recall who it was, but our brotherhood feelings came into play and we quickly cleared that mess up. Whoever wanted to start some stink had to chill out…and, of course, we won the game, plus we had on uniformed shirts! JABO RIMS! Player Coached by Joe L. Mack. They were not the prettiest shirts, but pretty shirts never sank any jump shots.

Joe Mack Reflects:

This was never more evident than the day the Rims traveled down to Long Island to take on a team of players that had several established all-stars and college players. They had come together to form a team on the Island to play in a league that summer and were looking for some outside teams they could play to help keep them sharp for the league. The Long Island team (I don't remember their name) heard about the JABO Rims from White Plains through a common friend and figured that would be a nice little tune-up game for the week. When we were told about their status and that they wanted to play us, we jumped in our cars and headed to Long Island. Only to find this team was already on the courts with fancy warm-ups and matching sneakers looking like a group that had just come from the Ruckers Playgrounds in the Bronx!! Our jerseys were a little shabby and faded, but they matched, and we had hand stenciled our numbers on them because, coming out of Winbrook, we didn't have extra money for the fancy stuff. Our shorts were mismatched, and you can forget about the shoes. I don't know what some of our brothers were wearing! Finally, we tipped it off, and the game was underway. Ernest Saunders dribbled the ball up the court and passed it off to James Coram, who pump-faked and kicked it out to Eric Rhodes in the corner for a jumper. Coming back down the court, Long Island threw in a lazy pass which was picked off by Don McLaughlin, who passed it to Joe Mack, who hit a trailing James Coram with a "no look" for a finish under the basket. After about 15 minutes or so, the score was 14 to 6 Rims! Then one of their star players got hot and hit 3 or 4 baskets in a row to tighten things up for a while, but that's when Cliff Livingston, Freeman Beville, Johnnie Randolph, and Kenny Cain went off. Needless to say, what we thought was going to be a long day on the courts ended up in a comfortable win, sending the Rims back to White Plains with another victory.

The JABO Rims played and beat all comers that year, ending the season with only one defeat which occurred in Mt. Vernon, on the 3rd Street playgrounds.

The Mt. Vernon Allstars vs the JABO Rims!

In order to set the stage for this epic battle, we first need to look at how it came about. Joe Mack was working the night shift for a payroll processing company named ITEL on Westchester Ave. in White Plains at the time, and he had a coworker from Mount Vernon they called "Taboo." Joe and Taboo would often work throughout the night discussing any and everything that came to mind to keep themselves amused during these long night shifts. One night the subject of high school basketball came up. Joe hadn't played on the high school team, but he knew most of the players from his days of playing with them on the courts at the Winbrook playground.

Taboo lived in the 3rd St. apartment complex in Mt. Vernon, where many of the Mt. Vernon players grew up, so he had a connection with them as well. Joe and Taboo spent several days going back and forth about which school had the better players while naming various people who played and who could stop who from the opposing school. We should keep in mind that while White Plains High was strong in basketball, football and track, it was mainly known during that time for its dominance in the arenas of track and field and football. Mt. Vernon High, on the other hand, was known for its dominance in basketball, producing college scholarship players year after year, many of whom ended up playing on the professional level in the NBA and abroad.

The discussions went on and on until the conversation shifted from "who was better back then?" to "who would win now?" approximately six years or so after their high school playing days. Taboo still knew how to contact many of the former Mt. Vernon players, and Joe, along with Jamal Koram, had recently formed the JABO Rims Summer Basketball team composed almost entirely of former White Plains players from Winbrook and the surrounding areas during the same era. The stage was set, the challenge was made between Joe and Taboo, and they went about making sure the matchup could come about and that the players on both sides wanted to settle the score.

The tournament was to take place on a warm summer weekend in the early 1970s with two games being played, one on Saturday and one on Sunday, both at the 3rd Street playground courts in Mt. Vernon. While Taboo rallied his troops, Joe and Jamal added the Mt. Vernon matchup to their summer schedule, and the dates were locked in place. What was about to take place would be legendary and would become the talk of the playground "fable" for years to come.

A team of Mt. Vernon's finest basketball players from their days of repeated high school championships were about to take on their old nemesis and rival from White Plains High, who hadn't often won their matchups during high school but always gave them a run for their money.

The day came and the White Plains players loaded up in cars that Saturday and headed over to the famed 3rd St. playground in Mt. Vernon. When they arrived, White Plains got a rude awakening to find that word had gotten around about this matchup, and the playground was packed with supporters for the home team! Not only was the playground full, but people were also hanging out of the windows of their apartments in anticipation of the start of the game and cheering for Mt. Vernon to put on a show. I believe they even had some cheerleaders if my memory serves me well.

Unnerved, the White Plains players emerged from their cars and approached the playground. We brought the best we could muster for this event knowing, it was a once-in-a-lifetime matchup, two of Westchester County's top high school basketball teams, coming together some five or six years after high school to finally settle the score.

Walking through the crowd to represent White Plains were some of the best ballplayers that have ever played for the school, Don McLaughlin, James (Jamal) Coram, Bill Cain, Eric Rhoades, Cliff Livingston, Freeman Beville, Kenny Cain, Johnnie Randolph, Ernest Dimbo, and Steve Washington, supported by several playground stars like Joe Mack, Morris "Cowboy" Green, Ernest Saunders and Willie Foster.

Across the court warming up for Mt. Vernon was an equally intimidating group headlined by some of the greatest players ever to grace the court during their high school run. Players such as Earl Tatum, Ray Williams, Rudy Hackett, Gus Williams, Al Skinner, and Mike Young stood ready with the rest of their squad to take on the challenge.

The game began, and neither team would disappoint the crowd. It was a back-and-forth battle for the first half, with both teams exchanging the lead with never more than a few points spread between them. In the second half White Plains got off to a quick start and we put up a lead of about 8 points early, Mt. Vernon stormed back and closed it to 2 but, thanks to the intense defense by Don McLaughlin and the others, we were able to sustain and win the game by about 3 or 4 points.

The crowd, which heavily favored Mt. Vernon, was clearly disappointed but remained civil and found solace in the fact that the rematch would be held the following day. White Plains showed up again on Sunday with several lineup changes to compensate for people who weren't there, only to find that Mt. Vernon had made some lineup adjustments as well. They seemed to have gotten bigger, stronger, and deeper as they stepped on the court and begin to play with a vengeance!

Again, it was a hard-fought battle with players raining threes from both sides of the court. The defense was intense as well, leading to Joe Mack and Ray Williams getting into a confrontation over a blocked shot. This quickly subsided and was put to rest when Gus Williams switched off on Joe Mack to defend his younger brother and landed a thunderous dunk over Joe on the following play! The crowd went "wild," and all was right with the world again for Mt. Vernon.

Now, with the home team leading by about 10 or 11 points, it began to look like Mt. Vernon was about to blow White Plains "off the court!" However, led by the defensive resolve of players like Ernest Saunders, Don McLaughlin, Joe Mack, Morris Green, and the rest of the crew, White Plains was able to hold them in check and allow our offensive weapons like Eric Rhoades, James Coram, Cliff Livingston, Kenny Cain, Freeman Beville, and Steve Williams to get us back in the game. It turned out to be a close finish, but Mt. Vernon ended up winning by about 4 points. The match may have ended in a tie, but the memory for those who were there that day will last forever. We now remember, reflect, and pay a special tribute to the members of both teams that are no longer with us, to say, "thanks for the memories" and may our brothers R.I.P.

j. v. basketball
back row: john newman, mike russell, john donahoe,
phil calabro, willis banks, manager: rick apfel, front
row: alan reisch, tom nathan, andy fredman, ed senas,
artie randolph, manager: rick apfel.

White Plains HS basketball Action Photo - Cliff Livingston taking it to the hole -
1969
White Plains H.S. Yearbook Courtesy of Cliff Livingston

Freeman Beville - Star player on the White Plains HS Basketball team - C.1980s
Courtesy of Cliff Livingston

CHAPTER 8

CARVER CENTER RECREATION, THE COMMUNITY ACTION PROGRAM (CAP) AND JOINT ACTION FOR BLACK ORGANIZATION (JABO) - IMPACT ON THE COMMUNITY

By Joe Mack

The recreation centers in White Plains have always been the hub where youth from all neighborhoods would gather to have fun in the afternoons and on weekends. The girls would come to relax and chat with each other while the boys would come to show off, play games, and try to "hit" on the girls, as in, use their rap game to see how strong it was and if they could get some attention.

Most often, they came up empty and could be seen later that afternoon walking back to the projects with a few friends and thinking about what could have been. During the time frame Joe Mack and Jamal Koram grew up, there were several key recreation hangouts, the basement of the Cage, just outside the boxing ring, The Carver Center located first on Main St., then on Lexington Ave. and later Fisher Ave., and finally, The Slater Center which came on as the others seemed to fade away and remains active until this day.

These centers provided a safe haven for the young folks from Winbrook and the surrounding areas to come together and spend time in a social setting that was both safe and a positive environment for them to grow. Much of this must be attributed to the adults who ran the centers. They saw to it that everyone remained respectful and would allow no foolish behaviors without the risk of being thrown out or even barred from the center for a period of time, which no one wanted to happen.

Some memories from Carver Center are the Friday evening social dances. Playing pool, table tennis, or foosball, and the occasional karate demonstrations performed by the amazing Sensei Mack, who would mesmerize the crowd with moves and techniques never before seen and then break into a deadly kata with "kai" sounds that could chill your spine and leave you frozen in your tracks.

Yes, there would be an occasional squabble, but it would always be taken outside after having a talk with one of the counselors and coming to some sort of agreement, which often led to both parties being willing to go their separate ways. Rarely was there a dangerous confrontation that drew blood or left someone seriously injured, again, largely due to the way the staff ran and managed the program, and they are appreciated for that to this day. They are to be commended for the way they handled, mentored, and interacted with the youth of that time.

There is, however, recollection of one incident that could have ended up being bad for several people had it developed any further. Gloria Rudd, who lived down in the Valley and was dating Joe Mack (Sensei Mack's younger brother) at the time, was being harassed every day after school by one of the guys she knew. Joe found out about this and came down to the Carver Center that weekend to address the issue with the person who was causing this harassment. The word got out beforehand that this was about to go down, and several people gathered to find out how it would turn out. Since Joe lived in the projects, one of his friends named Ricky Holdip found him and let him know the person he wanted to see had just shown up at the rec center. Joe and Ricky slowly walked up to the center and Joe told Ricky to go inside and let the person know he wanted to talk to him outside, but he also told Ricky not to come back outside because he didn't know how it would turn out, and he didn't want Ricky to be involved or get in any trouble.

A few minutes later the young man came outside, and Joe approached him to address the matter. The two engaged in a reasonable conversation that established Joe as Gloria's boyfriend and his request for the brother to show her the kind of respect she deserved by laying off the harassment. The young man indicated he didn't mean any harm and was just playing around with her, but he could see how she took it the wrong way. Both parties agreed that would settle the matter, shook hands, and parted ways.

It was then that Joe heard someone he didn't know ask the brother, "Is everything cool? Do you need us to jump in?" His response was, "Nah man, we worked it all out" as he walked back into the Carver Center. It was only later that Joe found out this brother knew about him and his brother, Sensei Mack's, reputations and had contacted a few of his friends from Greenburgh to be on standby that night. It was also discovered that at least one of them came armed with a weapon which could have turned quite dangerous for everyone if things hadn't gone the way they went.

Joe at that time was a skilled martial artist, a professionally trained boxer, and someone well on top of his self-defense skills, however, no one can ever say for sure how a confrontation will turn out whenever a weapon is involved, but grace prevailed that evening and no one was hurt after cooler heads were brought to bear.

The Community Action Program (CAP):

Growing up there were several positive outlets for youth to get engaged in activities throughout the community. One such outlet was The Community Action Program (CAP), and Joe Mack remembers getting a job in this organization along with several of his friends like "Bump" Robinson and a few others. Joe recalls working in the community passing out flyers and helping with the various youth programs around the city, it was one of my first jobs. This federally funded program is better described below in an excerpt from the study conducted on the 1968 White Plains High School Boycott entitled "Racial Confrontation" directed by Professor Dan W. Dodson, New York University, February 1969:

> "Another factor stemming from the community context is the development of the Community Action Program which was financed largely by federal poverty money. The philosophy underlying this program was "maximum feasible participation" of the poor. In addition to Ferris Avenue and East View CAP centers, there was a considerable program at the independent Carver Center. In all of these programs, there was special emphasis on the problems of the poor, especially the Negro. Mr. Offie Wortham was employed as a community organizer for the CAP program in addition to those who ran the centers." (p. 24)

Joint Action for Black Organization (JABO)

The Days of JABO:

By Joe Mack

During this period, James Coram and Joe Mack had gone away to college but both were back home for the summer and family visits. James attended the University of Akron out in Ohio, where he became the leader of their Black Student Union and Joe attended Westchester Community College in Valhalla, NY where, in time, he had become the President of the Afro-American Society on campus.

Some incidents of racial unrest spilled over from the late '60s and White Plains began to see an uptick in some discriminatory practices in the community, aimed especially at Black folks living in or around the Winbrook area. Joe Mack and James Coram became aware of several such incidents, one involving the White Plains Taxi Company and another involving a grocery store on Tarrytown Road near the bowling alley. They decided to form a committee to investigate these situations affecting the area residents.

Joe Mack and James Coram met with several other people from the community, and that led to the formation of JABO, "Joint Action for Black Organization." In addition to Joe Mack and James Coram, JABO was a group that included well-known people like Esther and Skip Washington, Ms. Elsie Harry, Eric Rhodes, and Cliff Livingston, among others.

JABO quickly sprang into action and formulated a plan to boycott White Plains Taxi, who had been disrespectful to a pregnant sister from Winbrook who was not getting out of the taxi fast enough with her groceries. This boycott ensued and was eventually successful in getting some demands met for better and more respectful service in our community.

JABO was also instrumental in another boycott of a local grocery store on Tarrytown Road. This store decided to fire a young minister, who needed some time off for church matters rather, than being willing to rearrange his schedule to allow him to meet his church obligation. After a few days of protest marches and the ensuing boycott of his store, the manager agreed to meet with the young minister to see if there were ways the schedule could be changed. We were well organized and peaceful but knew how to get things done without evolving into major conflicts.

CHAPTER 9

RESPECT: ELDERS, FAMILIES, AND COMMUNITIES

Respect for Our Elders and Others

by Joe Mack

During our years growing up in the Winbrook community, we had a tremendous amount of respect for our elders. We were taught by our parents to always honor and respect the elders that were doing their best to provide for us, teach us and protect us while we were growing up. Many of my friends, much like me, came from single-parent households, and believe me, it wasn't easy. We saw the day-to-day struggle by our parents to provide and to keep food on the table, and sometimes even the despair in their eyes, but they never let us feel downtrodden or give up hope. My mother, Ms. Mary Mack of 159, was one of the parents who kept a close eye on the behavior of all of us and was compassionately referred to as "Mom Mack" over the years. She was also a leader, along with Deacon Henry Williams and others, of the cub scout and girl scout troops in our neighborhood, who never failed to participate every year in the Memorial Day Parade in White Plains and to place flags on the graves of every veteran at The Rural Cemetery following the parade.

A faithful member of Calvary Baptist Church, Mom Mack wouldn't hesitate to correct a child from the neighbor even if it was the pastor's son. I could write a book about Mom Mack alone, but many others taught us to love and respect one another in our community. A few that come to mind are Ms. Rooke from 159, Ms. Williams from 33, Ms. Livingston from 159, Ms. Higgs from 159, and Ms. Harry from 135, along with many more. These ladies had a major influence on our lives and made sure we didn't stray too far from our upbringing. It was like that E. F. Hutton commercial; when they spoke, we listened.

There were several others throughout the five buildings who wielded the same measure of guidance and discipline for us, and we all knew who they were. Ms. Harry, for example, became an influential community leader and spokesperson when she stood up to the housing authority in a relocation dispute issue. She went on to represent many others in the same dispute matters and most often helped them win their case.

Even though each of the five buildings had its own unique identity, there was a common theme of respect throughout the Winbrook community. Don't get me wrong; it wasn't all good days and carefree living. We had our share of issues with drugs, crime, conflicts, and disagreements like any other project community in any other city in the country may have. However, there was a sense of a common thread of respect and compassion that ran through each of the buildings that was displayed with an unspoken code of dignity.

I can remember days when the hallways to enter the building would literally be packed with some of the brothers who had come in from playing ball in the playground and found this to be a convenient place to engage in any number of questionable activities. Maybe rolling some dice, drinking some Wild Irish Rose, smoking a little weed, or simply shooting the bull about the day's events. Despite being deeply engaged in these activities, if one of the elders pulled up after a long day of work or shopping for groceries, the crowd would stop whatever they were doing and would part like the Red Sea to make sure that the elders could get through. Not only would they clear the way, one of the brothers was sure to even help them get their groceries onto the elevator if any help was needed. This is the kind of mutual respect that stood out in my mind as I was growing up and was likely to be found in each of the buildings on any given day. Folks didn't always agree with one another or how they did things, but if you were somehow associated with Winbrook, you were awarded a certain level of respect on that alone and allowed to go about your business without harassment or conflict. It was understood that you simply looked out for one another and obeyed anyone's parents who spoke to you or corrected you in some manner.

CHAPTER 10

INFLUENCE OF CHURCIIES IN OUR COMMUNITY: SPIRITUAL AND RELIGIOUS GROWTH

By Joe Mack

Churches were a very influential part of our early life. Our parents made sure we got up every Sunday morning and went to church whether we wanted to or not. We later came to realize that in an environment where there were so many day-to-day challenges and most of the odds were not in our favor, the church provided a spiritual foundation and community bonding that was badly needed and couldn't be found in any other way.

Calvary Baptist Church - White Plains, NY - where Joe Mack and his family attended - photo 1980s

Like most communities around the country, there were several churches in or near the Black neighborhoods in the city, and White Plains was no exception. Churches like Mt. Hope AME, Bethel Baptist, Trinity United Methodist, Little Mt. Zion Holy, Calvary Baptist, and Allen AME, along with several others, provided the spiritual foundation for many of us growing up by helping to keep families and the community together. Pastors from these churches were instrumental in all aspects of our society. They often served as spokespersons for the Black community when addressing issues like urban renewal and family re-location. Some even served on planning committees overseeing the transition of businesses within the Black community and the selection of which areas would be targeted for renewal.

Most of the families in Winbrook and the surrounding areas attended either Bethel Baptist, Calvary Baptist, or. Mount Hope, with some opting for Trinity Methodist up on Fisher Avenue. My family attended Calvary during the time Rev. Phifer was the pastor so, I got to know many folks that way as well. We were also there through the years of Rev. Smalls and Rev. Cousins, while the church was growing, and new sections of the building were put in place. My mother was a very active church member who sang in the choir at Calvary Baptist, and I believe, worked with the ushers and several other programs in the church. I was even a member of the Male Chorus at about 17 years old myself and can remember spending time at choir rehearsal on Saturday evenings in the basement of the church. In fact, that's where I was on the evening that Dr. Martin Luther King Jr. was assassinated, and can recall the empty feeling I had inside when someone told me about it as I walked down into the basement. It was a feeling and a moment that I can never forget. Suffice to say, our spiritual growth started early. When something like that happens and you're young, you tend to process it differently. Emotions can range from sadness to anger, rage, and hate to confusion. That's when some sort of spiritual foundation in your life is needed most, and that's what being at Calvary Baptist helped provide for me at that time.

Calvary Baptist Men's choir under Pastor Phifer - Joe Mack 2nd row 3rd from right.
Photo date 1968

CHAPTER 11

HARD WORK – SUMMER ACTIVITIES AND CADDYING AT THE GOLF COURSE

During the late 1960s, the most accessible way to work and make money was to caddie. Everybody had a favorite golf course to work at, and Joe's choice was the Ridgeway Golf Course. You had to get there early and sit in the caddie shack until your name was called. If you were lucky, you got out within an hour or two, but it wasn't uncommon to be there for three or four hours on a slow day! Just waiting and engaging in a little small talk with someone you knew.

Caddying was a mainstay during the summer for many of us, and the primary way we made money, to buy some sharp clothes and try to impress the girls. Joe Mack and James Coram made frequent trips to the golf course for this purpose, and they usually preferred The Ridgeway Golf Course over Westchester Hills as their place of employment. James was a little bigger than Joe and he looked more imposing, so he generally would get called out first, leaving Joe to sit there with his peanut crackers and chocolate Yoo-hoo drink and wait his turn.

All the guys from Winbrook showed up there at one point or another. It was not uncommon to find people waiting in the caddy shack like Cookie Legg, Eric "Coon" Livingston, Ernest Bimbo, Johnnie Randolph, Eric Rhodes, Cliff Livingston, Frog Jordon, James Coram, Joe Mack, and many others on any given day. You can imagine the pressure on each of us to make sure we got to go out before our friend to have a better chance of getting a double 18 loop (carrying two bags for 18 holes) and getting a bigger tip! Caddies were paid about nine dollars a bag, and you always hoped to get two bags when you went out for the day to complete your loop and make the day worthwhile.

There were several memorable caddying experiences, but one that stands out is the day things were going slow at Ridgeway, and Joe decided to go across the street to Westchester Country Club to see if he could stand a better chance of getting out. Joe had never caddied at Westchester and didn't know anyone there, so he was a complete stranger. His home course, Ridgeway, was fairly diverse and a little less fancy than Westchester but, what the heck, he decided to give it a try anyway.

The first shock for him was opening the door to the caddie shack seeing no Blacks at all except for this one brother sitting way in the back by the Coke machine. That person turned out to be a young man from Greenburg, NY, next door to White Plains, named Billy Sudderth III. Billy was into bodybuilding at the time and had muscles popping out everywhere! All Joe remembers is seeing this "huge" brother sitting there with his forearm resting on the Coke machine like he owned it. Joe didn't know if he did or not, but nobody was going over to get a Coke, even though it was hot that day and everybody looked thirsty!

Joe went in and quietly took a position against the wall with a few others shortly before this other white caddy, who was also powerfully built, started challenging everyone to a match where two people would lock fingers together and press upwards until somebody gave in. Nobody was taking him up on his challenge, so he eventually walked over to the new guy, Joe, and asked if he wanted to try. Joe didn't know the game but felt that being new, he'd better at least take his turn in the ring. Moments later, they were locked in a fierce battle that ended with Joe coming out on top. The room fell quiet, but Joe now felt like he had gained a little respect to build upon. The big brother in the back, Billy, gave Joe a look that expressed his surprise at the outcome, but also a sense of gratification and approval.

Also, as a youngster, Baba Jamal remembered working until 2 am with Darryl Cole and his father cleaning offices and factories in Port Chester and Connecticut. Then he would have to get up at 5 am to go help his brother-in-law deliver newspapers, then off to his main job, caddying or school...talk about working hard!! Don't let anyone tell you that young Blacks are lazy and don't want to work. There were many other examples of the brothers from Winbrook working to help ends meet in the community...more, so many more...

Joe Remembers Other Notable Events:

Memories from the summers would include hanging out at the playground most of the day on the courts or just joking around with the fellows. Once in a while, there would be a special challenge that normally started with trash talking and ended being settled on the court.

Other highlights included the Show Mobile battles of the singing groups from the area, such as the Societies and the Sensations. James Coram was the lead singer for the Societies, while Irving and Bump Robinson were co-features for the Sensations. These two groups offered some classic showdowns with many performances in the courtyard that will be long remembered by those in attendance.

Additionally, we spent time at the Carver Center playing games, shooting pool, and playing ping pong. The Slater Center had not yet opened, but it eventually became the place that continued Carver's Center's legacy as time went on. Then there were our weekend trips to Saxon Woods swimming pools where it seemed that everybody showed up to swim or just hang out. In addition to White Plains, you had folks from Greenburgh, Mamaroneck, Port Chester, New Rochelle, and pretty much anywhere you could think of in and around Westchester County.

Joe Mack recalls one of his earlier trips to Saxon Woods came as a dare he made with several of his friends that involved proving who was the best swimmer. That Saturday morning, the fellas were gathered at Billy Walker's house, as usual, when someone mentioned that the only one brave enough to go off the diving board at the deep end was Billy. Joe decided to chime in and say he could do it as well, which led to an immediate challenge for him to prove it.

There was one small problem; Joe had experienced a "near-death" incident when he was a small child in a lake one day and since that time was terrified to go back into the water, so he never truly learned how to swim! Just the same, here they go, on the Mamaroneck Ave bus heading out to Saxon Woods with Joe sitting on the seat trying to figure out if there was any way he could get out of this ill-founded challenge he'd just made. There was no respectable way out, so when they arrived, Joe stepped onto the board, took the plunge, and to his surprise, resurfaced, and was able to swim his way back to the edge!

Joe's courageous act that day reintroduced him to the water, subsided his fear, and eventually led to him joining the US Navy. This just shows what we have within us sometimes, if we are willing to trust that we have the spiritual bonding to connect to it.

CHAPTER 12

DANGEROUS TIMES AND DRUGS

Joe Mack Remembers:

It seems that drugs began to take a foothold at Winbrook around the mid-'60s. Most people had become accustomed to getting someone old enough to buy a six-pack of beer, and everybody would sneak off into the back of the playground and pass the cans around until they were all gone. Back then, it seemed like Schaefer, Coors, Rheingold, and Ballentine were the brands of choice.

I didn't like the taste of beer and didn't often partake, but at around 14 years of age, I was one of the taller members of the group, so every now and then, they would ask me to go into the Italian store on the corner and buy the six-pack for the evening. There was also the occasion when somebody would show up with a quart bottle of Colt 45 and of course, he would be the kingpin for the day!

Although it was not a good thing and should never be encouraged for young teenagers to run around drinking beer in the parks and playgrounds at night, I knew of no one who was taking drugs or bringing anything like that to the group. That all changed when drugs began to filter into White Plains from the City. Certain people were set up or connected as the suppliers with a mission to get as many people "hooked" as possible.

Things began to change and people you knew and hung out with began to die as the result of an overdose or bad reactions to a chemical they had consumed. Reefer was also gaining increased popularity during this time and impacted its share of the community but not with the devastation and life-changing effects of the "hard stuff."

Despite all of this, the residents of Winbrook somehow managed to weather the storm and keep a strong sense of community. Parents like my mother became increasingly strict, forbidding us to engage in any of these kinds of behaviors or to hang out with anybody known to be messing around with drugs. The penalty for disobeying these rules could likely lead to a good "thrashing," as Mom Mack indeed ruled her household with a Golden Fist!

Baba Jamal:

There was a time in White Plains and in other cities up and down the east coast and elsewhere that drug usage swept through like a hurricane. At first, it was something to try. Then, like its predecessor, alcohol, it swept through Black communities like a plague.

Seriously. The sad thing about its arrival in poor neighborhoods was that it aimed at the youth. Most of the old heads stuck with their liquor and wine. The young ones fell in love with dope. At first, it was a more senior thing, but it quickly spread to older teenagers, and then the younger ones were introduced to it. All communities were hit with this plague, especially in the projects.

And it wasn't just boys. Late in the game, some girls tried it too. But in the early days of dope, youngbloods tried something that eventually would not leave them alone. Some of our age mates that we never thought would get involved in drugs of any kind, let peer pressure and "coolness" maim their lives. Some died. Others were addicted, and others faded away.

Fortunately, for those in the Winbrook neighborhood, we had a "savior so to speak," who knew how to revive those who had taken too much or whose bodies couldn't handle the drugs. We had an Angel, Kenny Mack., who KNEW how to SAVE folks LIVES. Those in the beginning stages of an overdose, or who were overdosing if he got to them in time.

What it boiled down to was that you had to stimulate the systems of those who took too much or took any at all and he DID save folks' lives. I was there a few times. One of the main things that had to be done for males, was to put enough ice on their scrotums to stimulate the blood flow… I was there three or four times assisting him. He saved all their lives. Primarily because the drug hadn't infiltrated their systems yet. There were a few that were too late to even look at …We wept for them and pray for their families, even to this day.

Kenny was like a good grandfather for all the young bloods. Wise before his time. A protector. He made me alert and ready, always challenging. Always present and never backed down from anyone with his five-foot, "I can knock you out...self." he made me alert and taught me how not to back down either.

Liquor was ALWAYS a problem, particularly in some low-income neighborhoods. It wasn't too much of a difference in Winbrook. From pre-teens to grandparents. But then, new drugs entered. As if we didn't have enough problems with liquor, and marijuana, and such. But heroin and a new batch of drugs hit home hard! Damn. Every other day, someone was losing a son.

They were older sons at first. But when we lost our first young teenager, it was more than too much to bear. Seriously. We were all in the hallway when the elevator door opened. Young blood spoke and smiled, and then he slumped down on the elevator floor. "He's on that stuff!" "That brother too young to be on that mess."

Some young brothers, maybe Otis Moore, and them, ran out of 159 looking for help. I believe he was trying to find Kenny Mack, while the young brother from Winbrook was slumped down in the elevator, barely breathing.

We called out for someone to call an ambulance. A couple of us saw him slump down, headfirst, then his whole body, and we knew that this was more serious than everyone thought. Some of us had seen this before, but not with one so young. "Somebody get Kenny!" "Get some ice!" "Call an ambulance!" No small cell phones back then...A couple of us helped Kenny with the ice. He was known to revitalize Bloods who made the mistake of thinking this was like wine or candy. This is straight-up death. And here we were, with a young one, tears flowing for him and his loved ones. Some of the Brothers were on the lookout for the ambulance. Others tried to walk him, but it was too late.

The first O.D. death of our peers. He had some other siblings as well. Decades later, the images from that episode still bring tears of sadness for family and friends …and regret that we never really knew who else was involved… it is just as well, for more families and friends, would have been weeping.

He was placed on the grass where the medics could reach him quicker. But we already knew. And we wept, as I am doing as I type this. Fifty plus years later. So why include it in this memoir? Because sacrifices were made in the names of our young! Be it this, or be it going to war, or be it dropping out of community life… pursuing other lifestyles, and we are still going through this mess, and madness that plague us. Even today. We knew it when he slumped down on the elevator. But you never give up on the ones that you care about and love as a community of families

We hadn't given up with the ones from 135, 159, 225, 11, or 33. The deceased, the dying, and the ones barely living. The alcoholics, the needles in the arms, the drugs as recreation. NO! And these weren't the only ones. There were more. No, he wasn't the last one. And the love for him was so great. Who introduced him, and the others to this junk? All we could do was put out a warning… but addictions set in quicker than do-gooders could respond. Folks on the street were making money. Some were making Big Money. Others were barely making it because they were using up their "profits "getting high or dying. May God Bless those who have asked for it. Since those times, many have asked for forgiveness for what was done or failed to be done. Others have had to battle their feelings over decades. God Bless our Memories, for what we did, or did not do… May they shine the light of love, understanding, peace, and joy on extended families, and life, and love…At sixty and seventy years old, and such, some of us are still crying… Seriously. We are thankful for the lives that were saved…

Love is the Answer.

CHAPTER 13

LAW ENFORCEMENT AND TRAGEDY

By Joe Mack

The mysterious death of Bennie Bennett

It was a cool summer evening like many others when everyone was hanging out in front of building159 having fun. Bennie was always a high-strung and fun-loving individual, but man oh man could he talk some trash! Bennie seemed to have something to say about almost everything and never backed down from a good argument.

On this night, I wasn't there, but the story goes that Bennie was in a back and forth screaming match with somebody when two white police officers pulled up and intervened. Supposedly Bennie began screaming at them as well and they decided to arrest him. Fast forward to the next morning when we all found out that Bennie had died overnight in his jail cell from an apparent suicide. Now we all knew Bennie, and the one thing we knew he would never do is kill himself. This led to one of the first protest marches held in White Plains, and to my knowledge, Bennie's death remains a mystery to this day.

The Shooting and Recovery of Sensei Mack

Another neighborhood tragedy occurred when my brother, Sensei Mack, the local karate teacher was shot when he attempted to break up a drug ring in Poughkeepsie, New York that was affecting some of his students. Rather than alerting the police in that city he decided to confront the drug dealers himself and was shot point-blank multiple times.

The story is told that when the paramedics arrived after receiving a call of gunshots in the halls of an apartment building and entered the side door, they encountered a man walking towards the exit. The officer stopped him and said, "Hey, I'm looking for someone who may have been shot," not realizing the man he was talking to was the actual victim! After being hit several times with injury to his stomach, chest, face, shoulder, and head, Sensei Mack was unable to talk but reportedly, just opened the front of his suit jacket so that the officer could see the smoke from his burning flesh!

Only then was he rushed to the hospital and into immediate emergency surgery, where the doctors were ultimately able to get him stable enough to receive the fluids, he would need to sustain life. I was in the Navy by this time and stationed in Norfolk, VA, but once I got the word, I was able to get there within hours of him coming out of surgery. I remember driving up to Poughkeepsie, walking into the lobby, and taking the elevator up to the seventh floor. I asked one of the nurses which room my brother was in, and she said, "He's at the end of the hallway, but there's a lot of people in there with him."

When I walked into the room, I saw my mother leaning over the bed holding his hands and crying, I saw my cousin, Bae Mitchell, and one of the karate students, standing next to her for support. I saw my brother's head karate student, black belt Bahru Seward, standing not far away and maybe several others, like black belts Rahku Lynk and Rasheen Reed in the room as well. The next thing I saw, miraculously, was my brother lying there covered in blood, which they had not yet been able to prep, with his eyes open!!

I walked over to the other side of the bed and grabbed his hand. He wasn't able to speak, but he gave me a slight squeeze to let me know that he was alive and would pull through. The sight of him lying there in blood with tubes running all over his body yet being aware and alert enough to squeeze my hand to let me know he was ok, was too much for me to take. I had to walk out of the room for a minute to gather myself.

I don't remember much more about that day, but there's one thing that speaks volumes and will always stick with me. On my way to the room to see my brother, I walked past another room where a young man, maybe in his early 20's was laying on a cot bleeding. Not being sure where Sensei was located, I stopped and asked the young intern what happened. He replied that the man on the cot had come to the apartments looking to buy some marijuana and when he realized they sold him a fake bag of lawn grass he tried to grab his money back and was shot once near the back of his ear with a 22 pistol.

Why was this so significant to me? My brother, on that same night and around the same time, was hit up to 19 times in various parts of his body with a larger caliber bullet, 32 or maybe 38 caliber, which normally would mean instant death, and the outcome couldn't have been more different. On my way back to the lobby, after spending some time in the room with my family, I noticed the other room was empty and the intern was cleaning up. I asked him about his patient, and he told me the other young man didn't make it.

Those who know me well, know that my spirituality is among the strongest parts of my character makeup, and my faith is unwavering. That night I pondered how a man shot once could die while another man shot multiple times on the same night could live, except by the grace of God and purpose.

Sensei was later transferred to Grasslands Hospital in Valhalla, NY, and I rode in the ambulance, taking him there. They rolled him into emergency, still with staples in his chest, while we waited for a room to be prepared for him. I then remember my brother tapping me on the shoulder and saying, "Look." I pulled back the sheet covering him and we both were able to look past the staples to see his intestines protruding out from the wound. My immediate thought then was "what kind of man is this that can look at his own intestines and smile?" Over time, and after multiple surgeries, Sensei recovered and went back to teaching karate at his school on Ferris Ave. If you're having a difficult time believing there is a power greater than anything that you can conceive, then you be the judge of what I just shared.

A Police Shooting Gone Wrong

Joe later read about a resident of 135 S. Lexington named Mr. Chamberlain, a former US Marine, being shot to death by police in his apartment while struggling with medical issues and possible PTSD. Joe didn't personally know this resident himself, but when he talked to friends and relatives, he found that Mr. Chamberlain was well known and well thought of by many people in the community, including Grandmaster Shihan Mack. This shooting made national headlines and was covered on all the news networks, with many different accounts being told about what happened that night but the end result is that another life in the community was lost in a shooting by a police officer who likely could have handled things differently and, if so, Mr. Chamberlain may have been alive today.

WINBROOK YEARS COLLAGE

Sensei W. Mack, Universal GoJu School of Karate, White Plains, NY Destroys a block of ice with his head in a city demonstration. Photo 1970s

Slater Center Scout Troop gathering in White Plains - 1980s

White Plains, NY High School basketball team - late 1960s, White Plains H.S. Yearbook, Courtesy of Cliff Livingston

CUBS-SCOUT OF WHITE PLAINS
WESTCHESTER-PUTNAM
C.O. CUBS SCOUT

Cub Scouts Pack 283 the youth Bureau of W.P. Meeting at Slater Center every tuesday night at 7:00 pm...... Chief Henry Williams Coordinator Mary Mack Club Master Also Mrs Rialey Den Leader. & Willie Mack- Weeblo Leader ages 8-10	Girl Scouts of Westchester Putnam County, W.P. troup 1980 - Brownies 1981 - Girl Scouts - Mary Mack-Troup Leader-Mrs Rialey Assist. troup Leader all at Slater Center 2 Fisher Avenue Meeting every Wednes- day at 6:00 pm also Lyna Lucas Coordinator of W.P. girl Scouts..... Call 428-5695 both for cub Scouts & Girl Scouts.

Slater Center Scout Club meeting announcement - 1980s

White Plains High Varsity basketball team around 1968, Courtesy of Cliff Livingston

Cliff's brother Eric Livingston playing for
Job Corps 1968 in Wisconsin,
Courtesy of Cliff Livingston

Joey The Ice Cream Man- served all of
Winbrook for decades date unknown -
Courtesy of Cliff Livingston

**Baba Jamal's Uncle Thelma lived here
- Greenburgh**

House Baba Jamal lived in as a child

The front of 33 Fisher and back of
159 S. Lexington Ave.

225 Grove St. - now MLK Blvd
- from the street

**Entrance 11 Fisher Ave White
Plains, NY - one of the five**

**The grounds where 135 S. Lexington
Ave once stood. 11 Fisher Ave
In the background**

Remnants of 135 S.Lexington Ave White
Plains, NY
and side view of Bldg 159.
Could it be next?

What used to be the Spanish store
across from
159 S. Lexington Ave in the '60s

The playground is now the staging area
for construction at Winbrook.
A view of where the courts used to be.

The laundromat still stands. This is where Sensei Mack
held some of his early Karate classes in White Plains
during the 1960s.

Building 135 S. Lexington Ave in White Plains, NY
- Gone but not forgotten.

Joe Mack - US Navy Master Chief - photo 1995

**Jamaroh Kai Mitchell and her scout troops
- Downtown White Plains, NY photo 1980s**

**Gamal Mack #75 and the White Plains Patriots
photo date 1980s**

Chief Henry Williams (2nd from left), Mom Mary Mack (5th from left) and others with the Slater Center Scout Troop in White Plains, NY photo 1970s

White Plains, NY Memorial Day Parade Photo 1980s

Joe Mack (left) and Vince Wilson traveling to White Plains, NY Photo 1980s

Slater Center Scout Troops placing
Flags for Memorial Day. White Plains,
NY Photo 1980s

Joe & Thelma Mack's wedding - Honors detail - Greenwich, CT. Left
to right - Sensei William Mack (Joe's Brother), Bahru Seward, Joe
Mack, Billy Sudderth III, James Coram, Rasheen Reed Photo Jan 1983

**White Plains Scout Troop in front of the
Slater Center - Full Dress for the occasion.
Photo 1980s**

CHAPTER 14

RACIAL UNREST OF 1968-1971 IN THE COMMUNITY AND THE HIGH SCHOOL PROTESTS

By Joe Mack

Racial unrest in White Plains High:

First, let me talk a little bit about some of the problems that were taking place in and around White Plains and especially up at the high school. James Coram and I both graduated in 1968 and, through some strange twist of fate, came to be very close and began to hang out with each other during this time.

This grew into a lifelong relationship that sees us as brothers to this day. We both knew each other from the playgrounds on the court and from caddying together at Ridgeway and some of the performances around town by the Societies, but it wasn't until one of our counselors, Mr. Pollock, took us down to Chinatown one weekend to take our SATs together, that we really became close.

James was one of the stars on the basketball team, a cool brother who knew how to make everybody laugh; a fun-loving brother who always knew how to keep everybody upbeat and in good spirit, one of his many gifts. He was also well known and respected throughout the Winbrook community for his gifted and talented ability to sing and perform on the stage with the Societies, a group that went on to achieve regional prominence and local fame for their show-stopping performances in White Plains and throughout the City.

I was rather low-keyed and spent most of the time hanging out with Ricky Holdip from 225 Grove St. Ricky was kind of a high-strung brother who had an engaging personality, and he was always cool. I also hung out with Kenny Cain from 11 Fisher, Kenny Mack from my building, Stuart Dotson from up on the Hill, Morris "Cowboy" Greene from down on Lake St., and several others from around the projects, when I wasn't playing basketball with the team from JABO.

The year we graduated White Plains High was composed of approximately 25 percent of Black students who generally got along well with the white students on campus. However, during 1968 racial unrest and riots began to break out in New York City and Newark, New Jersey, which resulted in several of the schools in the City having confrontations among their students. It wasn't long before this unrest spread to schools in Westchester County, namely New Rochelle High, Mt. Vernon High, and, yes, White Plains High.

I can vaguely recall all the demands we made, but clearly remember peacefully gathering on the lawn in front of the admin building in protest with the rest of the Black students and meeting in the hallway with the principal and superintendent to discuss our demands. The one demand that stands out to me was the lack of Black history courses at the high school level, and this was one of the main points of contention during our discussion with the principal and superintendent in the hallway in front of the office that day.

This discussion seemed to be going reasonably well until someone in the back of the group threw a quarter and hit one of the administrators, I think it was the superintendent, in the head. I don't recall who threw the quarter, but it ended our discussion immediately.

Some of the leaders representing the Black students were Glenn Rogers, James Myers, James Coram, John Fox, and Barry Bennett. These were mainly the students who spoke on our behalf during that period of unrest at the high school and were the ones who led the follow-up discussions in the school's auditorium.

My last recollection was that the principal spoke to us at a meeting one day following several days of negotiations and said that because we were too far into the current school year, nothing could be done to impact the class of 1968. However, he assured us that Black history classes would be included as an elective for students to select the following year. This seemed to provide some consolation, allowing many of the Black students to return to class from the lawns outside, and he kept his word. The following year, 1969, was the first-time students could choose to take courses in Black History as one of their electives!

Once we began working on this book, Baba Jamal and I traveled to White Plains and met with Librarian Ben Himmelfarb, from the White Plains Public Library. Once he realized who we were, he made us aware that we had been the subject of an earlier study describing the racial incidents that occurred in 1968. This study was directed by Professor Dan W. Dobson, New York University, Center for Human Relations and Community Studies, covering the Racial Confrontation at White Plains High School and was published February 4, 1969.

The following excerpt is from the study done by Professor Dobson which describes how some viewed the "Community Action Program" for their involvement with the students during the protest.

Many in the community believed that this program (...CAP) was responsible for the Negro youths' staging the boycott. They point to the speed with which the staff of the agency came to the campus once the disturbance started. Others contend that the negotiations stemmed from some source in the program. One person, more deeply involved with the youths but not connected with the centers, said she observed a discernible trend during the summer of 1967 for the boys to "leave off horsing around and become more serious." She said they had started reading the works of Malcolm X and Stokely Carmichael. She indicated that what was bothering them was related basically to their very identity as human beings. She said one could sense that they were changing from carefree youths to sober perplexed people.

The staff and the members of the board of CAP thought they might have had a little to do with the disturbance since they had been trying to involve the people in the solution of their problems. Some of the board members said they would have felt very complimented to have been responsible for it but doubted if they had that much influence through their program. (p. 24-25)

This study clearly listed the student demands as follows:

STUDENT DEMANDS:

While the singing of freedom songs and the recital of grievances continued in the auditorium that afternoon, the three student leaders meeting in the principal's office with administrators produced a list of demands. These were:

1. Black history course at the high school level.

2. Assemblies every other week featuring Black speakers, with all students required to attend.

3. Instant implementation of Negro representation on the senior prom committee. (Discussion revealed that there had been Negro students on the committee and this demand was then abandoned.)

4. More Negro books in the library.

5. Negroes to be employed in the cafeterias since none are now employed there.

6. More Negro teachers and guidance counselors. (The charge that guidance counselors were slow to move on any complaint was reiterated.)

7. Humanities class should be open to all.

8. White teacher attitudes must change. All teachers should be required to attend summer courses in human relations.

9. The schools must teach about Blacks in all phases of the curriculum. (p. 12-13)

    Agreement Signed:

    The agreement was:

    We the undersigned, meeting on April 3, 1968, discussed student grievances as follows:

1. That Negro history be integrated into the total curriculum.

2. That there be assembly programs scheduled for regular assembly periods with speakers and performers on Negro history and culture.

    We have mutually agreed that:

1. As soon as, in the judgment of Mr. Donaghey and Mr. Woodard, tension is down

in both the High School and the community, assemblies will be held under their direction and with the consultation of the student leaders and that there will be another meeting on Wednesday, April 10, to discuss the implementation of assembly programs, assuming that tensions have been reduced.

2. The three leaders, namely, James Myers, John Fox, and Glenn Rogers, with an administrative staff member, will be given an opportunity to meet with all students to discuss this mutual agreement. (Date to be worked out.)

3. We will meet periodically to discuss the progress and implementation of our programs.

4. On April 22 the Administration will give a definite answer as to whether Negro history and culture will be integrated into the curriculum for 1968-69.

5. The student leaders will do all in their power to establish communication with the administration and to help reestablish order.

6. The administrative staff will do all in its power to establish communication with the student body and to reduce tensions within the community.

James Myers   Manson A. Donaghey
John Fox   Principal, White Plains High School

Glenn Rogers   Daniel A. Woodard

Carroll F. Johnson   Director, South House
Superintendent of Schools   White Plains High School (p. 19)

Innovations Resulting from the Incident

A number of steps were taken immediately at the high school to give evidence of administrative good faith and to rectify those deficiencies in the program which could be remedied in short order.

The student leaders had originally requested that they have some kind of meeting of all students to make their position clear. On April 10, it was decided that the social studies classes could meet in the auditorium for this purpose. Arthur Bruesewitz, Social Studies Department Chairman; Mr. Woodard, Mr. Ivers, Mr. Binotto, and the student leaders addressed these meetings. The leaders presented their case and answered questions posed by members of the social studies classes. The consensus of the administration was that the sessions were worthwhile.

Lunchtime and evening elective seminars were instituted with the assistance of John Harmon of the Westchester Chapter, Association for the Study of Negro Life and History. (p. 59)

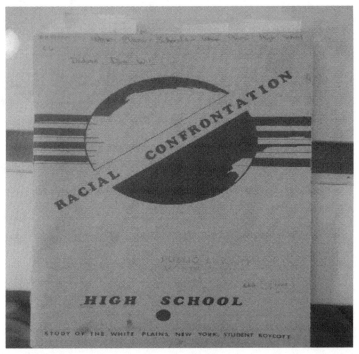

Copy of the study done on the student boycott in 1968 at White Plains High School, White Plains, NY c. 1969, White Plains Library White Plains, NY

The Freedom Schools of 1971:

Joe Mack

During my conversations with Karate Master Bahru Seward of the Universal Goju Ryu Kai School in White Plains, he recalled riots that later broke out at the high school in 1971. He remembers that it all started from an incident in the lunchroom after temperatures had been rising between the students for a while and were almost at the boiling point. When Jimmie Reed, who later became Karate Master Rasheen Reed and Jimmie Harry were confronted by the administration and told to calm down, they felt offended and refused to follow this direction. This incident, according to Master Bahru, turned into a full-scale riot where fights broke out, chairs were thrown, and people had to run for cover. When things were finally settled, the Black students left campus and were not allowed to return. Master Bahru, who by this time had become the spokesman for the students, recalls that since the students could no longer go to class, the seniors would be in danger of not graduating that year. He said after several community meetings, the Black churches in the community such as Trinity and Mt. Hope, along with a number of others, came together and formed "The Freedom Schools" so that the students in their neighborhood could continue to learn. As it turns out many of them would still not be able to graduate that year and had to attend night school at Eastview Middle School in order to meet all their requirements. Master Bahru credits dynamic night schoolteachers like Coach Smith, Ms. Cynthia Adams, Ms. Brown, and Mr. Woodard for helping them to pull through and leaving lasting memories for them all. The Freedom Schools were conducted in the churches for the period of time the students couldn't go to class and, is remembered by all who graduated with the "class of 71."

Bahru Seward (on the left) - one of the spokespersons for the 1971 White Plains
High School Riots - with Joe Mack, White Plains, NY - photo 1970s

CHAPTER 15

THERE'S MUSIC EVERYWHERE

By Baba Jamal

As a singing group, Bump Robinson and his group, the Sensations, came together and battled it out with the Societies at a "Battle of the Bands" at the County Center. The Societies had singers and a band from Winbrook and Greenburgh. It was a wonderful contest and competition, regardless of the outcome. The Societies won, but everyone had a good time.

As a result, the Societies went to the next level of competition at the Rye amusement park, where they battled it out again against other bands from the county and won. The prize was to perform on a float at the Macy's Holiday Parade in White Plains, the Westchester County Seat, and home!

Back then, our world consisted of several major neighborhoods in White Plains: The Winbrook Housing Projects, The Valley/Silver Lake, Ferris Avenue, and Battle Hill (that's where those giant twin brothers lived). I don't remember where they played basketball, but they went up to a college in Buffalo, NY, later to play college ball. I bumped into them once or twice when I was handling business in that area. It's always good to see home folks when we come home or when we're out on the road, whether it's two years or twenty years of absence.

Beyond those areas, once outside of Greenburgh and Elmsford with Tarrytown headed southwest, and then south and southeast, there was Yonkers, Mt Vernon, and New Rochelle, which were north of the Bronx in New York City. Northeast you'd find Port Chester, Rye, and Mamaroneck. On the other end, back toward the river, going North, it was Ossining and Peekskill as far as Black communities go, and beyond that, it was Poughkeepsie and upstate New York. Years later, Jamal would end up living in

Poughkeepsie and making a good name for himself. This city was across the Hudson River and seven miles or so from New Paltz College, where a few folks from Winbrook went to college.

And there were other times, including the "Show Mobile." The Show Mobiles performances, and of course we supported the events, including the marching parade events on Main Street, and Mamaroneck Avenue. And the races around the circle in front of "33." We know that Winbrook Pride isn't about gender, it is about families and friends. (See the Memoriam page for the departed ones we remember, here or departed. Amen.)

However, the majority of our times, outside of school, and school activities were with the fellows… and the majority of our thoughts were with the sisters… "Sho you right!"

"Not on The Outside" by The Moments

Y'all remember that song?

It was one of the cover songs, sung by The Societies. They were our homegrown five-piece singing group, and five-piece band, that lasted a little while. The band and one singer, Bobby Jackson, were from Greenburgh. The other singers were from White Plains: Darryl Cole and George Young were from 135 in Winbrook, Chuckie Addison was from 33, Winbrook, and James Coram, from Wyanoke Street. That was the White Plains crew. The band came from Greenburgh. The original band was: Louis Archer/drums, Reggie Life/Lead Guitar, Lloyd Reed on Bass, Billy Sudderth on trumpet, and Greg Dawkins from Valhalla, was on xylophone. Did I forget somebody? Oh yes, and Earl Cole on the conga drums. This was the first of a few groups Darryl put together that represented the main talent from White Plains.

The Societies won the Battle of the Bands at the County Center, in the semi-finals, against our crosstown brothers, The Sensations, Bump, and them from Ferris Avenue. It was a close competition for sure. The Societies also won, at the competition in Greenburgh, against some local Rock Bands. After that, we won the Westchester County Battle of the Bands at the amusement park, Playland, in Rye Township. As a result, our group was also invited to the Westchester County Thanksgiving Day Parade in the Westchester County Seat, White Plains. And of course, Winbrook was represented in addition to the Societies, with our White Plains High School/ "Winbrook side of town" Majorette sisters, and if our memory is correct, there was one brother among them from Winbrook, all leading and marching in the same Thanksgiving Day Parade! Both groups showed out. It was a prideful time for Winbrook…and for all the families we represented at that Thanksgiving Day Parade…from Tarrytown to Elmsford to Greenburgh, to Port Chester! And White Plains …WINBROOK IN DA HOUSE!!! Didn't James Coram sing the lead on the song: "Cowboys to Girls? …" Didn't we ALL show out, in the Thanksgiving Day Parade in White Plains? Wow!

All of these groups preceded the days of a younger band from Greenburgh called the "New Band" who went on to eventfully move to California and became famous as Atlantic Starr. This group became known worldwide for their melodious sounds and harmony as they recorded major hits such as "When Love Calls," "Send for Me," and "Catch a Four-Leaf Clover," among their many hits that moved up the charts in the '70s and '80s. They brought fame and recognition to the entire region, putting Greenburgh, White Plains, and all the surrounding areas musically "on the map" so to speak.

James Coram and Joe Mack knew the original members of Atlantic Starr best and hung out with them from time to time, whenever the occasion allowed. The group was made up of the Lewis brothers (Jonathan, Wayne, and David), Porter Carroll, Billy Sudderth, Koran, Joey Phillips, Clifford Archer, the lone female singer Sharon Bryant, and their manager, Earl Cole.

At one point when The New Band was just getting established out west in Los Angeles as Atlantic Starr, Joe Mack, and James Coram made a cross-country trip to California and decided to look them up. They had a brief, but wonderful, reunion with Joe getting destroyed in ping pong by Billy Sudderth and Joey Phillips, before heading down to San Diego where, by this time, he was stationed in the U. S. Navy.

The last group Darryl Cole put together that I was a part of, included brothers from the Bronx, and Harlem, NY. It was called COME and was managed by Earl Cole, Jr. who, after we broke up, went on to manage Atlantic Starr from Greenburgh (that's another story).

At that time, I was commuting back and forth from SUNY at New Paltz for rehearsals in our Bronx studios, performances in New York City, and up and down the east coast. Darryl Cole, Earl Cole (Manager) (135) and I still represented Winbrook …In fact, one summer we were on the Show Mobile Summer Talent Tour with presentations at Winbrook, Ferris Avenue next to the Summit House, and at a park near the Valley. I remember that well because we sang an old Temptations song; "I Wish it Would Rain" and it did!

The storm chased much of the audience ONTO the Show Mobile stage! We just kept performing and had a good homecoming time. I can remember the Moore family from the Summit House, on that day, with the whole family including Mama Moore up on the stage. New rain brought new times.

And during that time, there were a few of us from White Plains, who attended SUNY New Paltz College together. As a result, our singing group had the opportunity to open for a Gil Scott Heron Concert at the College. And we showed up and showed out. Whew! Did I tell you about the time Earl Cole and I went to one of the "Latin Theater Shows" in the Bronx on a Saturday night to see Ray Baretto and the All-Stars and ended up driving to New Orleans… and back in time for work on Monday morning?

Back to the Carver Center. In those days, the Carver Center was about a block or two from the train station, and right across the street from the White Plains Taxi Cap stop, and "Boss Record Shop", before Charlie and Maime, moved it further up Main Street. Whew! Years later, after Charlie passed, Maime established the shop in the train station. It was good for me to see her there, they had lived in the same building as my sister and her family, right off Battle Hill. I believe we were upstairs, and they were downstairs. We are thankful for all the memories of "45s" on the turntable…

Boss Record Shop
by Baba Jamal

Every week
Looking for the latest
At Boss Record shop
Spinning around, spinning around
Kurtom, Tamla, "45s" and some new song Charlie would put on the turntable:

Spinning around, spinning around
Charlie and Mamie Yates
45's in the '60s change is in the air…
Main Street/spinning around, White Plains

Spinning Around, spinning around
Never thought too much About 40th Birthdays
Gray hair and dying.
Now, 50 is young, and Curtis, Marvin, Ester Phillips,
David, Paul, Melvin, Otis and Eddie…and Martha Reeves and the Vandellas …
Are ancestors

And Charlie's gone too
Love to Maime and the family…
We all taking it to the next level in time and place
And space and Spinning Around…
Do you remember that time and place?
I knew if I saw you
I would lose my gray hair cool
I knew If I saw you one more time
My mind would nudge my heart
And I would be
Spinning Around, spinning around…
no, no why did we ever stop…

I hope you have slow danced closely
and stayed in love again, and again, and again
Or, like me…visualizing at least one more time…
Ouch!

Actually, when the Societies and Ferris Avenue's Sensations, met in a battle of the bands at the County Center…. Our only regret is that there were no pictures of the event that we know of. If there were, I sure would like to see them. It's a shame we had to be challenging each other before we could get together and perform WITH one another. From the parades to the Show Mobiles that summer, in addition to our nightclub, and other acts…The Societies were on a roll and well-loved. We are forever grateful for Home area love.

I do remember well when the Sensations came on stage at the County Center, we had already performed. I've forgotten the song, but they came on stage right, moving to the music, and one by one they dropped to their knees, and "knee walked" onto the stage, and with another move, came to their feet real smooth and timely. Those were fun days. RIP those who have gone on. The performers and the audiences… Amen.

And we have to apologize that the memories are not balanced between male and female…partly because we didn't "hang out" with sisters as much. Of course, we had many female friends and shared memorable times, i.e., races around the circle, family cookouts, and House Parties up Fisher Avenue, is that Lafayette Street? And then there was the Carver Center Rec Dances, and later 'upstairs/45s record parties, and at the Circle, and up on Ferris Avenue. And of course, H.L. Greens, with all the Brothers on one side, and all the Sisters on the other side, and when the slow jam came on, it was like a herd of Buffalo running to get to the someone you wanted to slow dance with all night long. And later on, I'm gonna tell it like it was! LOL, OUCH! What a memory…

CHAPTER 16

THE DAWN OF DISAPPEARING

By Baba Jamal

CHANGING TIMES:

During the late 1960s, THINGS were changing beyond the drugs, and strangers appearing from out of nowhere, and the new pipeline to Harlem, Midtown, and Downtown Brooklyn, and the Bronx. Folks were packing up and moving. A "Ball of Confusion" was rumbling. Folks coming back from the war, wounded, with changed personalities, or some didn't make it home at all. Love and Blessings…R.I.P.

This was only the beginning …

Around the early seventies, colleges were more available, and were accepting more minorities, and were releasing more financial opportunities to get scholarships and such. Drafts into the military and prisons were in greater demand…there were good job opportunities, in distant places, away from home and out of state. Who was staying home? Old fathers, and grandmothers, and others who had graduated from liquor, and gone on to chemicals and such, to meet death… sooner than expected. What were we doing? Why didn't we see this coming? If we did, what could we have done differently? Maybe we could have come back home with our degrees, knowledge, ideas, and such. But the providers, distributors, and the sellers didn't get us all. Some stayed and fought in the undeclared war against the "Black and low income." Against the weary and the poor. Against those of us living on, and in some cases owning prime land. Quiet as it's kept. There was strong resistance in some places. A good fight, despite the losses. Yes, we lost more and gave more to horror, and tears, and bad/sad news from home, and abroad in the war. But everything must change.

Many karate organizations began to pop up in the city and those karate organizations caught on. In cities and towns "new bloods" came back to the old neighborhoods they grew up in! These folks were determined not to go out in sorrow. Old entities, and organizations, and churches were still holding on despite interruptions by the devils, of all colors, and wealth sizes. There was something inside of the many, that didn't allow them to give up, or to accept failure, or not to believe that cycles have endings, but that they have beginnings too. We prayed and prayed for conscious New Beginnings. Yet, no matter how much knowledge we had, or prayers we prayed, we knew, we could only fight for scraps …and scraps, more often than not, are easy to shovel, and can be used up, or destroyed quickly.

Our community atmosphere was eventually challenged by deliberate raids, deliberate narcotics entries, deliberate shut down of social events, and gathering places. The welcoming and allowing of drugs, alcohol, and negative presence knocked us back quite a ways. And quickly. Gone! Let us be clear about who we are and what we require. A lifestyle waiting to be born in another place and time. Not far away, but ours. The lands have changed hands, but there is still land yet to be developed, protected, and saved. Wherever our people live. Let us not succumb to a short-range crap game.

Our time, our movement, our understanding, and our long memories, not only suggest that we awaken ourselves… but to awaken ourselves to LONGEVITY. It is making a DEMAND for life and community! For those whom we cherish and love, let us not give up or give in. Which means, at the very least, that we must seek to educate, motivate, stimulate, and designate. At least. May we teach and learn how to designate, and claim what is for us, and keep, and protect what is ours!

In the name of "Bump" Jerome Robinson, this must be done; by some group, someone with some wealth, and desire to do so. Baba Jamal has talked to at least two brothers who are capable of helping to preserve the memories of Brookfield St., Martine Avenue, Lexington Ave, Fisher Avenue, Grove Street, Dennison Street, Post Road, Main Street, Battle Hill, Ferris Avenue, The Valley and all the rest of those hills and valleys that we called HOME!

Back Before the Summer of 2020: Before the FIRST BRICKS Fell:

"Demolition Now". - Before the first bricks fell at 135 So. Lexington Avenue, White Plains, NY.

Back before wine turned into whisky, and whisky, into powder, and powder into needles, and needles into funerals and such. Powdered drugs ended lives. Before folks started walking around with masks on their faces …and it wasn't Halloween, and it only helped a little bit before we realized the warfare we were in, there were more dying on "death beds" in hospitals, than were being discharged. And it goes back further than that.

There was always an "exterminator" running around taking people's health, and destroying families, and the difficulties we had in our Winbrook days, with bringing up children, and families, struggling with finances and togetherness, and at the same time, working on community improvement and such. As conscious folks, and community residents, we had our hands full!

Some of us stayed, but Winbrook populations were dwindling. There's a war going on! "Everywhere." Young men were either leaving to fight wars, or to go to jails, due to narcotics, and its lifestyles; and to inner-city violence, or not returning from either. Less folks, less frequency on the basketball courts, or on the playgrounds. Churches losing males and family memberships. Yet, bars, and hustlers, and cowardness, were seeping into project elevators and seeping into project apartment homes, and crippling young children's understandings of life, and familyhood, and righteousness. Those who knew were dying off. Moving away. Those still here kept praying and working toward family, and community, and the resurrection of "home." As my Aunt Creola (South Carolina- RIP) used to say, "Thank God, for life."

Before the Winbrook bricks were being hit, and fell, and for opening our minds and enabling our families to be stronger. Despite the military drafts, the weapons on our walkways, the mindless departures of close ones, and the drugs…We heard the blessed voice of the Creator, enabling us to rebound, regather, recreate the careless mistakes we made, which were not small mistakes at all. We've asked for forgiveness, assistance, resurrection, for many things, and God's mercy and the love of our Winbrook families have forgiven us and like other activities in life, you either danced with death and got sick, and/or useless and mean; OR you got quiet on a route to a slow life departure. Escaping an unfinished life. We paid a price in our hearts, our homes, and our lives. Yet, we are thankful that many of us corrected, and have forgiven ourselves, our parents, our siblings, our relatives, and our friends; before it was too late. And What is Next? Is there a "next" around here? Remembering that this land is our land too. Yet! If not here, where? Keep your eyes open. Keep your mind alert. Seek others, who have been seeking you.

We had a chance to apologize; to ourselves, or others; a chance to say "I'm sorry" to relatives and friends; some here; many gone, and to ask for forgiveness. Or to forgive. Things we should have done decades ago, but maybe it's not too late, if we are all still here, reading this?

Having moved to other geographic locations, returning to Winbrook, in time to see:

The first bricks of destruction fall: 135 South Lexington Avenue, White Plains, New York 2020. Stands no more, only in memory and spirit.

Here we are, decades later, and we will never forget family workers, working endlessly to keep family life real and to secure family by working, going to two or three, or more jobs, coming home late from one job, leaving early to another. Coming home, getting some sleep, before awakening to this work cycle. Too often, this would lead to a slow separation from your wife, your daughters, and your sons. Yet, some of us focused, "Strong Ones," overcame that crap. They were the focused, determined mothers, children, and fathers, dedicated to being family; protecting their obedient children, and helping their true friends, and neighbors, when they needed a helping hand, or a kind word, or a prayer. Among other places, and other people, it happened in the five buildings, this was the real Winbrook. A gathering of neighbors in five, nine-story buildings surrounded by neighborhoods with food stores, churches, barber shops, and salons, car dealerships, a Hospital, Bars, Dry Cleaners, a Military Recruitment Office.

When the rubble falls, and we have secured bricks for memories, recognizing the past, present, and future of Winbrook… let us be clear…some folks we will never see again, (at seventy, too many of that era already, we grieve) and in the decades of separation, we have already crossed that bridge, not with all, but with TOO many …but we will have told their story. We will have remembered some good times like when Mr. Cole in 135, would pull up in a company van in front of 135, and picked his son, Darryl, and I up in the company truck, and we would go to several office buildings, and factories, in Port Chester, and then Connecticut, and do a quick clean up job, emptying trash, dusting desks, spot mopping the offices, or in the huge factories we would empty the trash, straighten up and jump in the van to go to the next client. We were back at Winbrook, about two in the morning, and I was at Wyanoke Street, getting up at five a.m., to deliver papers with my brother-in-law. Then off to our regular jobs or school, I don't remember which…

We will have shed tears, remembering some friends and foes, and some not-so-good times. Hopefully, Joe Mack and Jamal Koram will have cast some smiles, and said, "Thank You" to ancestors, families, and friends, and to the Most High …. Amen.

During one of our last trips to White Plains for interviews, the COVID pandemic was beginning to take a foothold in the New York Region. New Rochelle, NY was one of the first places in the country to have a major spread of the virus. The city of New Rochelle had begun to shut down and quarantine an entire section of the city to limit and control the spread of the virus throughout the area. New Rochelle is about 15 or 20 minutes from White Plains, but White Plains hadn't been affected much at that point.

While driving up the New Jersey Turnpike enroute to White Plains, Joe Mack and Baba Jamal took the occasion to reach out, and touch bases with one of their close friends and colleagues in Virginia, Leah Stith, who is a powerful figure as a community leader in her own right. Leah is also director of the Sankofa Cultural and Learning Center in Portsmouth, VA, and was surprised to receive the call.

When we told her, we were on the way to New York to conduct interviews for our book, the first thing she said was, "Have you all been watching the news? Are you crazy? New York is shutting down because of COVID!" We assured Leah we were taking all safety precautions and would also avoid going to the New Rochelle area…we all shared a good laugh about our adventurous spirit in the face of this developing pandemic.

The trip went well but ended abruptly when the White Plains Library decided to reduce the risk involved by canceling the space, we were allowing for interviews the following day. We were scheduled to interview Jimmy Harry but had to leave the area before we had a chance to reach him.... yes, the virus was getting bad, and our trip had to be cut short, so we never got a chance to talk to Jimmie. We also called Alden Mitchell on that trip, but unfortunately, had to miss meeting with him that day as well. His farewell, as we crossed the Garden State Turnpike South was "I love you brothers." We shared that the feelings were mutual and that we would see him when we came back home with the book.

It was during this final trip we met in the Slater Center with Heather Miller, Hurvy Bradshaw, Anita Roper, and Jan Mayzack to discuss plans for a book signing in the coming months. The group made us aware of a festival in White Plains that would also serve as a reunion and unveil a play, directed by Jan Mayzack called, "If These Streets Could Talk". Jan Mayzack still lives in bldg. 225 to this day and was as excited as we were about this joint effort. However, COVID derailed all of our plans for at least the next year or two and placed everything on hold.... delayed but not denied, we pushed on to the finish line!

We all knew that it was coming one day. In fact, many of us thought that the demise of Winbrook was overdue. There was a time in the last few decades, where it seemed like things were falling apart, physically, mentally, upkeep, etc. But never Spiritually. Even though, like other cities, White Plains' Black communities appear to be fading fast... It was hard to believe, at times, the standards of life some folks had chosen, and sunk to.

Winbrook was and is Home, Hope, History, and a "Mecca" for some families, and local employees.

Mama Mary Mack, Shihan William Mack, Coach Joe Mack, and Gamal Mack 159. The Mack Family have a South Carolina Heritage, as does Baba Jamal. Whereas, on the other hand, there were others who had faith and hope. Hope, not only for a better life but for peaceful living. Winbrook has had many years of a good life...as well as some years, not so good.

"But Winbrook Pride...never died..."

In every DOWN situation, there are always two or three UP situations to balance it to some degree. Be it some Long Standing Churches (LSC), or new Churches, or day care facilities, or individuals having parties in their basements, and individual families holding it together. Maybe it's just SPIRIT! Spirit meaning, having a sense of home, hope, and spirituality, visions… and Karate!

CHAPTER 17

LASTING MEMORIES: WINBROOK EXPERIENCES AND BEYOND

Baba Jamal Memories to Behold
Winbrook Neighborhood Stories 1960 – 1975
Five by Nine
five buildings - nine stories

Brother Coram …Remembers

Greetings, this is Uncle Sam: We're talking about the recruitment of young men primarily, to enlist in the military, enroute to the Vietnam War. The letters came in the mail, with those words, and mandatory instruction as to what to bring to the recruitment office. Basically, a toothbrush, maybe a washcloth, and the "invitation" letter you received in the mail. I received mine and showed up at the recruitment station on Post Road and Grove Street (now MLK Blvd). It was a full bus that carried us from the recruitment office on the corner of Post Road and, to the military building in New Jersey.

A few weeks before this, the recruitment building in NYC was trashed and destroyed by protesters of the Vietnam War; and closed down. So, recruits rode to Newark, New Jersey on a passenger bus. The bus was packed, as we eased onto Post Road, headed south, on the way to be enlisted in the military. Some of us knew of each other, so when we disembarked from the bus in New Jersey, we hung out together. There were about 15 of us. We just walked around, until we were called in to take a physical, and if we passed, we would be enlisted and assigned to a unit.

That was the last day some of those brothers were seen. As I told you before,

I walked with a limp, from a head-on bike and car collision on Tarrytown Road in Greenburgh in 1963, but it didn't deter me from being one of the best basketball players in the county, nor did it prevent me from doing labor work. The crooked leg and facial and scalp scars didn't deter me from any activity, sports, manual labor, or slow dancing. Fast dancing too!

Anyway, I was classified 1Y following my physical exam "To be used only in time of war…" Vietnam was not classified as a war, so a crackhead brother, whom I didn't know, and I, were the only two returning to White Plains that day. I still weep for those brothers I rode the bus with on that day and the others who didn't make it back home… We are thankful for the returned…some were wounded and changed, mentally, but home, nonetheless. Amen.

But I digressed from the storyline …while at the Army recruitment center in New Jersey. We walked back from our slight episode with some limousine bodyguards, who had driven up in a long limousine. Anyway, we backed up, and just walked around outside, until we were called in to get a physical, etc.

I came home, had multiple work opportunities, some janitor jobs, newspaper delivery, etc. until I enrolled at Pace University in downtown Manhattan. You see, ever since I was eight years old, I was a Ward of the state, on welfare, and had a caseworker. My caseworker was dedicated to her work. She stayed in touch with me for a while, even though I was no longer on welfare, and eventually assisted me in getting into another college after a one-year enrollment in Pace University. I was a good student at Pace, a starter and star on the freshman basketball team. I was also an officer in the Black Student Organization, but I ran out of funding and dropped out. I ended up working at the same IBM, where I had worked before on these large computers the summer before I started at Pace.

Now, Joe Mack had enlisted in the Marines, and went straight to the war front, as did Brother Cole, from 135, in Winbrook Apartments, and others from 33, 135, 159, 11, 225, and in the surrounding communities. I remember both returning home. What a joyful time for the families. It was Thanksgiving, and I was with the Cole family, who had moved to the Summit House high rise, up on Ferris Avenue. Mama Cole had a long history with my mother, Elease Sheppard Coram - Aponte', and with my paternal grandmother, Nettie Coram. Darryl, Earl, Jennifer, "Pops" Cole, and I had become close friends.

As for Joe Mack, it was another mother connection with his mother and my mother both being from South Carolina. So, he and I made that South Carolina connection stick.

Just reminiscing. For two years, or more, Coach J. at White Plains High School, cut me off the final list to be on the White Plains High School Varsity basketball team. Mike Hull, Freeman Beville, Eric Rhodes, Ron, and Herbie Moss, Glenn Rogers (my best friend …), and others, not only made the team, but would vouch for me, and did! They vouched for my basket-to-basket quickness, defense, rebounding, and my dunking abilities, etc. but it seemed like the coaching crew couldn't get past my bent leg and limping.

Well, one day after being cut for the third time in as many years, during lunch period, a few of us were in the gym. The players for the team had already been chosen for the team, and I wasn't one of them. A day or so after the tryouts, during lunchtime, we were all in the gym, and I was playing one-on-one with a player who was the chosen center when Coach walked in. I was playing one on one with one of the players he had chosen over me. The player was taller than me, about six-five, but couldn't jump higher than me.

Everyone was watching. I kind of felt sorry for the dude playing against me. Long story short, Coach walked in, and my homeboys let me know, and a couple of them were speaking playground lingo to me, that Coach was watching and my Winbrook crew edged me along. I stole the ball from the dude and dribbled it, that's when I heard one of my Winbrook boys call out "Dunk on him Loon, throw it down!" And I rose to the occasion and slammed the ball through the hoop! My lunchroom boys were in an uproar.

The lunch bell rang, I got my stuff. On my way out, I walked by the coach and heard him say. "If you want to be on the team, come to practice this afternoon." My brothers saw me getting ready to say some street stuff and calmed me down. I came that afternoon. And that's why I am with the team, in the 1968 yearbook. I did my share of playing for the school when I was called to do so (I should have been left in the Mt. Vernon away game).

That was proven a couple of years later when our Winbrook Summer Team, "New York Poles" faced some of the best players in the nation. We were up double figures at the end of the first quarter. My Winbrook Brothers were feeding me, and I was dealing! Mt. Vernon didn't know me! In the first and second quarter, Freeman Beville was hitting, Eric Rhodes was dropping those jumpers, making them, Mike Hull was sinking them long-range shots, and Ronnie Moss was setting us up. I was rebounding and hitting short-range jumpers. We were winning at the end of the first quarter. That's when I was taken out of the game, never to return…There was more to it than that. Let's talk about something else. Damn. And look, my Mt. Vernon friends sent me a picture of me that was printed in their high school newspaper.

(That was 50 plus years ago…But we're still crutching around, talking stuff and creating, that is, doing what needs to be done, as best we can.)

Dances on the weekends. They began early enough and ended late enough to do a lot of face and slow dancing, plus…Late enough to enjoy the company, either you came with, or that you were going to leave with, whether it was a group together, or walking behind the group on our way back to the projects. We somehow managed to show our feelings toward one another. And sometimes, it wasn't even about that. It was just having a good time and being good friends, like at James Myers house (Rest in Peace my Brother) in a group of friends…or at Irene J's, with good friends, good music, and good chaperones. Some of those friendships, and good feelings, I know, last to this day, some we haven't seen since the last party. But that's changed, thanks in part, to Facebook…no matter where we live now, 55 years later, for many of us; the images are clear, the vibes are good, and the love is strong.

But H.L. Greens Department store's upstairs empty loft, was where the party was, and it was always packed with teenagers, and those sisters couldn't get any finer!

My, my, my! And look, I recently saw a few of them on Facebook, and they are still fine! I don't want to get no one in trouble, I'm just sayin'. And dig this. For a while, I thought about dancing and such at H.L. Greens late, then I remembered running home to beat my curfew time. NOT. Those are the times that I really learned some things. Like, if you start late, you're going to be late. No matter how hard I tried, I was late, more times than early. And that was rough, because this was like maybe my third foster home, and I just wasn't getting used to that way of life.

After I recovered from a head-on collision car accident on July 4, 1963, at the time, my foster family, who was living in Greenburgh, had sold the house and moved to White Plains. Now, I was in the hospital from July 4th to November 22nd and I was released on the same day President Kennedy was killed. My social service worker picked me up from the hospital and drove me to White Plains instead of dropping me off in Greenburgh. Since only one family member, or friend, except for one person, the wife of the man who crashed into me visited me, no one else visited me...except for that Angel. In fact, no one else visited me the whole four months I was in the hospital. I didn't know they moved, and I didn't know they had not saved a sleeping place for me in this huge home and before I decided to run away from that situation, they still only provided me with a small seat in the hallway, as a sleeping place. I was belligerent, disrespectful, and ugly. I didn't like myself. I didn't like the fact that as I healed, I walked with crutches, and I hung out longer, etc. I threw pebbles at my sister Joyce's window so she could let me in late at night.

Well, that's enough of that, let me turn back to Winbrook. That's why folks saw me at the projects all the time, all day into the night. Whew! Got that off my chest!

Everyone who I had lived with had moved from Greenburgh. No one had visited me in the hospital except for the wife of the man who put me there. She visited regularly. I am thankful for that. And then this young girl came to the children's ward I was on in Grasslands Hospital. She was from White Plains. Her teenage sister would visit her, along with her teenage friends. They were a little older than me. They thought I was cute. I KNEW they were pretty! As I discovered later, they were all from Winbrook! 135, 159, and 33 and they later became my Guardian Angels when I was dropped off in White Plains. When I was out of the hospital and in White Plains, I enrolled in Highlands Jr. High. At the bus stop, I met "Downey Flakes" and his older sister, and guess who were the first students I saw when I arrived on crutches? YUP! All of the pretty sisters from the hospital who insisted on carrying my books and eating lunch with me. That is how I got to know the brothers. That's how I arrived in the big city, on crutches, with no fear, and plenty of friends, and I later found out, my relatives were all around me as well.

I think Darryl Cole, and Earl, figured who it was from their mother having known my mother. My family connections from the Valley caught on, but those five

173

sisters from Winbrook were my guardian angels.

Highlands Jr. High, where I would not have known anyone, outside of kinfolk…I was now introduced to the world of Winbrook Housing!

Homework and such was done in school. Yours truly was getting A's and B's, still moving from place to place, when I came upon the Mack Family. Now, in the projects, I had relatives and folks who knew my mother back in the day. The Cole Family in 135, treated me like family. My mother and the Coles knew each other from the time I was two years old when they lived on the corner of Martine Avenue and Brookfield Street. We reconnected when they found out who I was and were glad that Darryl and I had met each other. I also tried to reconnect with Eugene and Lorenzo Battle, we lived in the same foster home for six years in Greenburgh. They were my baby brothers, and nothing had changed in that regard when we all landed in White Plains on Orchard Parkway.

Brother Joe L. Mack -One of Mama Mary Mack's Boys

One of the Blessed Ones Returns from Vietnam

"What are we here for, except to remember, recall, revive, and relive?" Baba Jamal Koram 2020

Joe L. Mack came back from Vietnam wounded, healed, and commemorated. He is a military hero. The potential for great things has always been present in Joe Mack's life. You heard the stories from rural South Carolina, saw it on Spring Street in White Plains, and later in Winbrook Houses 33, and then in 159. Joe was and is respected, not only because his brother is a world-renown karate expert, or that his mother, grandmother, and caretaker to his oldest son, Doc, was a gracious loving individual respected by all…but Joe "Lukata" Mack is respected because he inspires goodness, has a helping hand, a joyous personality, and a sincere approach to friendship and life. Plus, he is an expert in any endeavor he embarks on.

THE NEIGHBORHOOD CONNECTIONS:

The White Plains Demographics:

White Plains is the County Seat of Westchester County

By Baba Jamal

There were four basic Black and semi-Black neighborhoods in White Plains. These were the Winbrook Housing Projects, the Valley, and Ferris Avenue and Battle Hill was the other one. Each had its extended surrounding neighborhoods.

For example, Winbrook had Fisher Avenue, Lexington Ave, Brookfield Street, Post Road, Denison, etc. Each of these areas were communities unto themselves, i.e., grocery stores, gas stations, schools, churches.

We probably should point out that Fisher Avenue did have its own park, which grew from a single basketball court (that Jamal used to practice on) to an outdoor full-court where a young blood took my legs from under me when I was flying for a dunk, and I fell on both my wrists. Anyway, the park had swings, merry-go-round, and such.

Outside of White Plains was Port Chester to the Northeast, on the Connecticut border. Mamaroneck, Rye, and New Rochelle to southeast/ Mt. Vernon to due south, and southeast to Yonkers more or less. Its close proximity to major areas in the state of New York allowed for opportunities in all arenas. Traveling straight west from White Plains, were Elmsford, Tarrytown, and Ossining, Peekskill et al which was aligned to the north riverside with the Tappan Zee Bridge, from Tarrytown crossing the Hudson River, into Nyack, and is one of the key doorways west. To the north, it was primarily Port Chester leading into the border with Connecticut. (For the sake of clarity, Greenburgh will be considered a suburb of White Plains.)

Other than those routes we had connections with the community and organizational events, events, in addition to sports.

In central Westchester County, there were other cities that were connected by sports, friends in some cases, and relatives. The County Center events, including circus events, graduations, cotillion events, championship County Wide Basketball Tournaments, professional sports events, and others.

Joe Mack, founder of the "JABO Rims Basketball Team," reminds us that there were popular athletes and sports personalities in other Westchester County cities and towns. Particularly basketball athletes. Cities like Yonkers, with Charlie Criss, in Mount Vernon with their basketball brothers, Gus and Ray Williams, Scooter and Rodney McCray, among so many others, or Brickhouse in Peekskill. If they were playing ball during that time; James Coram and other JABO Rim brothers had their own reputations in the county. Eric Rhodes, the Saunders brothers, the Livingston brothers: Coon, Cliff, and Eric Livingston, Ernest Dimbo, Bill and Kenny Cain, Johnnie Randolph, Freeman Beville, Ron Ross, and others…

Each neighborhood had brothers and sisters that had skills and ideas and character, and all that made cohesive communities. Living spaces that we all can be proud of, no matter what geographic, and despite mistakes made, or errors in judgment, etc. The bottom line is that most of us lived through it. We've given our lives to other realistic and helpful endeavors and with gratitude. Knowing that many of us are still here to represent a people, that is, a neighborhood, a community, a town, a city, a county, and a time that was full of change, sadness, some happiness, and hope. A time of happenings; some of which we know that we don't want to forget. More importantly…there was a "Time of Life" that we want to recall. Not everything, but definitely some people, places, and events, that we will remember. Stories, memories, people, places, and activities that we recall, and that we will pass on. We will not forget. God Bless us All.

May who we are, and where we've come from be remembered. May the love in our hearts for folks, past and present, during the Winbrook years. be sustained. This would include extended communities outside of Winbrook. Let the stories of Winbrook be told. Don't leave the planet with memories unsaid, with friends left unknown. Write it! Sing it. Say it. Play it. Review what you've read in this publication and PASS it on! This is how we continue from generation to generation. By being available! No lies necessary, the truth itself will bring enough joy, sadness, and laughter…and Winbrook Pride!

This is our story. Talk about it. Be about it. Add to it! No one can take away any of who we are, or what we have or have not been. How much we have or don't have…Leave the foolishness on the circus floor… (do you remember the circus at the County Center?) Everything has its place. The "Winbrook Years" contributors want to be sure that our stories, and those of others, are told for as long as we can. And as Brother Jamal Koram has suggested: May we "Remember, Rekindle, Reclaim, and Restore our People to their Traditional Greatness." Let us not forget who we are, who we want to be, and who does not have our best interests for life! We will know them by what they say and in what they do. "Power to the People!"

(Koram, Jamal (2020).

Baba Jamal's Memories to Behold

It's the year 2020

On a recent trip,

Joe and Jamal witnessed the final and complete demolition of the first project building of 135 South Lexington, the first building to go.

Several folks plucked bricks from the demolished building. Some of you all remember when Leroy, "Buckets" Smith threw a spiraling football onto the roof of 135! What an arm, and accuracy? Imagine how far that could go if thrown to Otis Hill, streaking down the sideline… horizontally. Wow! As we remember, Buckets didn't play high school football for one reason or another.

We remember seeing Brother Chuckie Addison getting that first baton at WPHS Track Meet. He had some basketball in him too.

And Look! Remember when activist, Benjamin, from 33 could dunk a basketball from a standing still position. It wasn't that he could jump real high …he had LONG arms! He was a straight-up activist-warrior, highly intelligent, and dedicated to whatever he put his mind to. It was thoughtful and good to talk with the brother, who always carried books, and, or black news/newspapers, and such. We had our differences of opinion, but no difference of reality, and necessity. What was his sister's name…?

And there were other athletic highlights in those years. Especially with the track team. But there were other highlights for sure, Like that championship basketball game, at the County Center, White Plains High School versus? If you were there, you would have witnessed when John Lee (33 Fisher) made a half-court bounce pass ending in a slam dunk by David Jackson (who played football, ran track, AND played basketball, as a few of the running backs did …) And still hanging on were the well-known heavy hitters but they were in trouble. Eric Rhodes, James Koram, Lawrence Mosley, Ronald Moss, and others. This was the "new" sophomore class coming on!

Baba Jamal Relives His Experience at the Penn Relays and White Plains Victories:

Baba Jamal:

Speaking of track and field, Jamal re-calls going to the Penn Relays, in Philadelphia, Pennsylvania, with "Aunt Margie", Glenn Roger's mother, him, his siblings, and his extended family. This is when I lived in a foster home with the Carter family, for a while, along with my adopted brothers and sisters. We all lived on Wyanoke Street. What a wonderful outing! My sister, Madge, would have loved to have made this trip, to see White Plains Track Team "tear up" the Penn Relays! Records were broken, short and long distances. These were our homeboys! And we were there to witness, and to be able to tell, because we were there at the stadium, In Pennsylvania!

The White Plains track team was destined to win the 4 x 4 relay, individual races, with power and "Tiger" pride. What made it doubly nice, was the fact that we were there, and that we knew ALL the brothers! We were blessed that day, not only because we knew the team, but that we could also visualize other team members that we saw at high school track meets, running on the high school track. Brothers like Chuckie Addison….

But here we were at the famous track stadium, and an annual track meet, seeing our Homies breaking records, accepting first place trophies, In the name of the Orange and Black! Davy Jackson, Otis Hill, Larry James, and Carl Reed and, there was a "fifth man" I can't recall his name right now… GOT IT! Cedric Thomas. Had anything gone wrong with the initial runners, he would have filled in.

Our College Days:

Baba Jamal

Alice Bowman, Steve Bowman, Cheryl Bowman (Greenburgh) and, Steve and Jamal Koram (J. Coram), were in colleges in Ohio at the same time…Stevie at Kent

State University, and Jamal at Akron University. Did I tell you the one about driving to Ohio late one night on the Pennsylvania Turnpike…When it was Stevie's turn to drive my Thunderbird, and after going through a toll on the Pennsylvania Turnpike, in the Mountains, we ended up with all four wheels off the ground, after paying the toll.

A car with six huge Caucasian football players, in the middle of the night, pulled up beside us in the Mountains of Pennsylvania …" Y'all boys need some help?" "Yea, if y'all don't mind …" They told us to stay in the car, then they walked to the front, back, and sides and lifted the Thunderbird off the divide, and set it down on the highway, got in their car, laughing, honking their car waving, with the power to the people fist in the air yelling "Power to the People…" maybe that part didn't happen? It could have, and I think it did.

We made it to Kent State with no further issues. And look, Stevie asked, "You wanna drive man?" "Hell no! I just finished driving through all those Pennsylvania Mountains! No thank you." And I fell asleep. I saw him once or twice afterward, whenever I would attend a social/or political get-together at Kent State. More the former than the latter. And haven't seen or talked to him since.

Dennis Silas - was my Ace and a smart brother. He was a ladies' man and was with me in the Disciples. Remembering when Downey, Dennis, and I were headed to Dennis' house on Post Road, and we saw some smoke coming from that direction, along with fire engines, flashing lights, etc. It turned out that it was his apartment that caught on fire. His mother had gone to sleep, and something was cooking…

Charlie and Ernest Silas - great ballplayers - JABO Rims!

Roderick Gray - a wild brother and a good ballplayer. He also considered himself a ladies' man.

Other Places and Thoughts:

The "Cage" on William Street:

Boxers: Kenny Mack, Herschel Jacobs, Cleo Daniels, Buster Douglas, Joe Mack, Eugene Battle (Martial Arts) and Lorenzo Battle: Baba Jamal's foster brothers (from the time they were three and four years old, 45 Washington Avenue, Greenburgh, NY).

Sixteen years young and still growing too fast.

Sixteen years old and still coming home, late.

Staying out later, despite basement punishment, and straight home from school, and extra chores …Trying to obey… to get along, but I stayed at 228 West 22nd Street, NYC too long, before a foster home with younger siblings than me, a curious mind that comes from unknown genius, and eight years old walking from 228 West 22nd Street through the Empire State Building and Grand Central Station after which, trying to find my way back to 228 West 22nd, but I digress. It is now 1966 and I am returning to White Plains, this time not in the "Valley" but off Fisher Avenue on the west side and Post Road on the East.

Joe Mack

Baba Jamal also remembers coming home from the University of Akron one summer and the two of us hanging out for a while. Bored and with nothing special to do, we decided to ride down to a nightclub in the Bronx on 233rd St., just to listen to some music and enjoy ourselves for a while. It was a weeknight, and the club wasn't too crowded so finding a table was easy. What happened next goes back a few years when Baba Jamal and I made a trip to South Carolina to visit family and, in an attempt to make a group of kids on the street laugh, Baba Jamal created what became known as the "What Can I Say?" face. This was an expression where he would shrug his shoulders high up around his neck, puff out his jaws and hold out his hands as if to say "what can I say?," which always worked and never failed to get a laugh!….now back to the club in the Bronx, while we were sitting there listening to music, a young lady came in and asked if she could join us rather than sit at a table alone. We obliged and a pleasant exchange of conversation ensued …what's your name? Where are you from? and the usual opening conversation for folks who didn't know each other. Everything was cool until a discussion of the "what can I say face" came up and she wanted to see what it looked like. I tried to warn her that it was created while joking around with some kids and was no big thing, but she insisted on seeing how it looked. After a moment or two of trying to discourage her, Baba Jamal said "ok, if you must, here it is." We all broke out into some healthy laughter and only then was it evident she had laughed harder than she intended and inadvertently revealed the need for some serious dental work… which only made the situation worse. Everybody from Winbrook knew it was never a good idea to challenge Baba Jamal (then known as Looney) to make somebody laugh! You would always lose because he was naturally a funny Brother when he wanted to be.

CHAPTER 18

WHITE PLAINS, GREENBURGH, AND MAMARONECK – JOINT EXPERIENCES AND RELATIONSHIPS

By Joe Mack

Greenburgh, New York is a town with a population of about 80,000 located right next to White Plains and separated essentially by the White Plains Bowling Lanes, a suitable line of demarcation for the two cities, where people from both locations often met. It stands to reason, then, that folks living in both areas developed close ties over the years to one another. You could almost say that White Plains, being the larger of the two, was looked upon as the "Big Brother" to the Greenburgh community and the two were joined together in many ways. White Plains High and Woodlands High schools shared many of their school and college experiences as well, keeping their bond into adulthood and even until this day. Greenburgh was somewhat of a quaint and peaceful place and home to several of Westchester Counties' celebrities such as Moms Mabley, Roy Campanella, and Cab Calloway to name only a few.

White Plains, on the other hand, was somewhat larger, somewhat more diverse, and the location of "The Winbrook Housing Projects," which was the core base and home for many of the Black families that lived in White Plains. You can see where this is going, it stands to reason that ties between the two cities were very close and that many of the Black families in Greenburgh had connections in some way to families in White Plains. They either knew someone that lived in Winbrook or had family members themselves living there. The interactions between the two transitioned quite smoothly, as there was a seamless stream of travel back and forth, especially among the younger folks. When thinking of the Greenburgh to White Plains connection, several people or families come to mind.

Mr. and Mrs. Archer had several sons and daughters, Louis, Bobby, Clifford, Janice, Helen, and Shirley. One of their sons, Clifford, was an original member of that world-renowned R & B Band, "Atlantic Starr," which got its start in the Greenburgh-White Plains region and went on to produce multiple hits including gold and platinum albums. One of their daughters, the late Shirley Archer, married my older brother, Karate Master Sensei Mack, and became my sister-in-law. She is also the mother of my niece, Kiana Kelly, who now lives in Florida and is an accomplished author and poetic artist in her own right. The Archers are long-standing Greenburgh residents, an amazingly gifted and talented family, who brought a lot of value to the community.

Two of Joe Mack's relatives - Kiana Kelly (right) and her daughter, Kayla Mack - Florida residents from White Plains - 2021

The James family, in the same manner, also made long-lasting contributions to the region. Another upstanding family of high integrity and purpose within the Greenburgh community and one of the pillars of the community to this day. Their son, Larry James, went on to attend Villanova University on a track scholarship after graduating from White Plains High School and later achieved immeasurable fame by winning a gold medal in the 1968 Mexico City Olympic Games during the time of protest for equal rights by Black members of the U. S. Olympic team.

The Lewis family was unique in that three of their sons, Wayne, Jonathan, and David were all among the original members of "Atlantic Starr." These extremely talented brothers rose to stardom on the heels of their success as gifted recording artists, writers, and musicians from yet another Greenburgh family that made major contributions to the entire region, placing them on the map at the top of the R & B charts.

The Sudderth family was another well-known and highly respected family within the Greenburgh community and one that became like my "second family" over the years. Everyone in the area knew of the Sudderth family and held them in very high regard. Mr. Sudderth was the first Black commissioner of the Greenburgh Fire Department, and also managed his own insurance company. He ran his office run out of his home, which was also impressively maintained by Mom Sudderth, an exceptional cook, and an avid reader. Mom Sudderth read so many books it would make your head spin just looking at them on her shelf.

The Sudderth family was seen as another of the pillars for the Black community in Greenburgh and played a role in key functions in the White Plains community that centered around Winbrook. Mr. Sudderth played the coronet each year in the Memorial Day Parade through the city in which my mother, Mom Mary Mack, proudly displayed her scout troop with their American Flags, on their way to the Rural Cemetery, where they were placed on the graves of every veteran.

My mother and Mom Sudderth also frequently visited each other and would talk about baking pies and other family activities.

Billy Sudderth III, the oldest sibling, is highly intelligent, creative, and a uniquely talented and gifted young man who took pride in bodybuilding, playing chess, and playing the trumpet. He went on to pretty much master all three of these skills and became one of the greatest trumpet players ever witnessed by the music industry as a member of "Atlantic Starr," after completing his time in the Marine Corps.

Billy and I really came to know each other well during our time in the Marines while going through Boot Camp at Parris Island and Infantry Recruit Training at Camp Lejeune. This is where we discovered we were both from White Plains and later grew to become the best of friends, only to later find out we were actually distant cousins who had a lot in common, we have maintained that lifelong connection to this day.

June was the oldest of the Sudderth girls and was someone who had a personality that could light up the room. Her pleasant nature and friendly approach garnered her a multitude of friends and acquaintances in school and throughout the community. June was the one her other siblings leaned on to keep things in check and to provide a sense of reasoning whenever needed.

Phillip was the younger brother and was always calm and laid back. His thing growing up was playing tennis and Latin dancing. Man, could he go...put him on a dance floor with the right music and the right crowd and Phillip would take it to another level. He brought the house down on more than one occasion with his fancy spin moves and smooth shuffles at several Latin clubs down in the Bronx that folks likely still remember.

Theresa was the baby girl in the family and was always taken good care of by her brothers and older sister. Tee was very smart and a gifted young lady in her own right, with a pleasant and warm personality as well. Following the patterns of her brothers and older sister, she could sing, dance, and flow with the best of them.

The Corams lived right next door to the Sudderth family and were another well-respected Black family in the community. Mr. Coram worked for the police department and his daughter, Carol, was a standout in school both academically and in track. They were relatives of my co-author, James Coram, AKA Jamal Koram, and we all spent time together just hanging out and catching up on the events of the neighborhood whenever we could.

Another significant connection to White Plains was Alden "Splouse" Mitchell who lived on Dobbs Ferry Road in Greenburgh. Alden and I became close the summer after High school when we both worked for the Urban League of Westchester's Voter Registration Program. Mr. John Harmon was the director of the program and, also a community organizer in White Plains who helped a lot of young Blacks get their start during that time. I was designated as the person who drove the van as we traveled around Westchester trying to get minorities in the community registered to vote.

Along with Alden and I, our team consisted of several impressive young ladies, Jane and Margo Green were sisters who lived in Wyndover Woods, Jennifer from Tarrytown, and Cynthia Blackwell who didn't live too far from the Sudderth family. Needless to say, Alden and I had a ball that summer driving through the neighborhoods in White Plains, New Rochelle, Mt. Vernon, Mamaroneck, and Port Chester trying to get people registered and trying to make the ladies with us laugh throughout the day. Alden was the prankster and I usually ended up being the target of most of his jokes!

Alden and I both went away to college after the summer but stayed in touch over the years and shared some pretty interesting adventures, like the time we drove across the country to California in my green Ford Mustang! We rode from White Plains to Detroit for an overnight layover and then headed west, following a big truck and talking to him on my CB radio all the way to Denver, CO. our next layover. It was White Plains through Ohio to Detroit, then Missouri to Kansas to Colorado where we encountered a couple of street hustlers and had to watch each other's back. Finally, we took it down through Las Vegas and on into San Diego. Man, oh man, what a trip! We were the dynamic duo, traveling partners from east to west.

Let me reflect for a moment on one of the most interesting connections between the Winbrook projects in White Plains and the town of Greenburgh and that is my co-author of this book, Baba Jamal Koram. Jamal was born James Coram and moved with his family to Greenburgh from New York City as a young child. He was fun-loving and very personable as any child would be but also faced a series of challenges growing up in Greenburgh during that time.

One of his most difficult challenges was being hit by a car while riding his bicycle on Tarrytown Road around the age of 12 or 13 years old. This accident nearly took Jamal's life and, as it was, left him severely injured and in a full-body cast for about the next six months or so in what at the time, was called Grasslands Hospital in Valhalla, NY. Though badly damaged physically and limited in his mobility, the accident did not dampen Jamal's spirit. He remained upbeat and positive about his recovery throughout his months long journey in Grasslands Hospital.

It was this positive outlook that befriended him with another patient from White Plains who happened to live in the Winbrook Projects named Anita Roper. Nita was also recovering from a medical procedure that required an extended stay and the two of them talked often about their recovery. Nita tended to get frequent visits from several of her friends at Winbrook, notably Pam Brey, Sandra, and Judy Valentine among several others. It seems all these girls took a liking to Nita's new friend and would visit him when they came up to see her as well. Eventually, they began bringing Jamal treats on occasion and started combing his hair to straighten him up a bit, seeing as how he was in a full-body cast and couldn't do any of that for himself.

Over the next few months, they grew close together as a group and the hospital visits continued until Nita was discharged. This relationship proved valuable to Jamal when he was finally released from the hospital himself and was re-located to White Plains. On his first day arriving at school, getting off the bus still on his crutches, he was recognized by the girls that he met in the hospital and they all rushed over to help him with his books and to make sure he got to class ok.

This was cool for Jamal since he didn't know anyone else at the time, but it also made the other brothers a little concerned about this new guy that was getting all the attention from the ladies. What's up with that? Who is he? Needless to say, things smoothed over as they got to know Jamal and found out how laid-back and fun-loving he was.

Sometimes great things come from humble beginnings. Part of what makes Jamal's journey so unique is what he had to go through from the start, being raised pretty much by his older sisters and foster parents as a small child, surviving a horrific car accident, and still rising to do great things later in life. Jamal eventually regained his health and leg strength, so much so, that he played on the White Plains High Varsity Basketball team and became one of the star performers and lead singers of a local musical group called the Societies. He was also one of the leaders of the Black student protest movement in the class of 1968, went away to college, and became the president of the Black Student Union while at the University of Akron and later, also at the University of Virginia in Charlottesville.

This all led to Jamal eventually being crowned as Baba Jamal Koram, "The StoryMan," and becoming one of the greatest African American Storytellers in the country. Our friendship spans from the days of high school and we have grown to become more like brothers over the years. Thus, when I reflect on my growing up in the Winbrook Projects and all the positive influences in my life, I couldn't think of a better person to help me collect the memories of those five buildings and the people we knew, admired, and shared these experiences with, than Baba Jamal Koram, "The StoryMan."

The Mamaroneck Connection:

By Joe Mack

Black families from Winbrook and beyond were always closely connected to other Black families throughout Westchester County; it stands to reason, then, that there was a thin line of separation between cities like Mamaroneck, Greenburgh, New Rochelle, Mt. Vernon, Port Chester, and Yonkers, to mention a few, with White Plains in that regard. Subsequently, people met and associated with each other in many different ways and through many different activities, such as sporting events, shopping at the malls, the movies, visiting their relatives, and sometimes just hanging out at the parks and on the courts.

First, there were Joe's adopted cousins, Johnnie and Kenneth Rush (KT), who lived with their parents, Aunt Ruth and Uncle Zeke, in Mamaroneck across the street from Carl's Bar. Johnnie and Joe were about the same age and knew each other from their days as youth when they grew up together in Sumter, SC. They were very close, almost like brothers, and hung out all the time until they both joined the military. Johnnie went into the Army after high school and Joe eventually joined the Marines. They stayed in touch, however, and always swapped stories about their different military experiences.

Dave Pemberton from Mamaroneck, NY was an outstanding basketball player at Rye Neck High School--1968 grad-- who knew many of the White Plains area ballplayers as well. Dave is now a dentist living in Richmond, VA and he can recall many of his "high flying" days on the courts and watching White Plains players like

John Lee, Ron Moss, Freeman Beville, James Coram, and Cliff Livingston dominate opponents in the games they played----whenever basketball was in question, Winbrook was always in the house! Dave later played college ball at Amherst University, but never forgot the experiences he had in White Plains.

Larry Albert from Mamaroneck, NY was also a graduate of Rye Neck High School in the class of 69. Today Larry still lives in Mamaroneck after completing a career as a Westchester County counselor for disadvantaged youth. He now works as an actor, model, and singer who has maintained his standing as a community activist. He often frequented White Plains and knew many of the Winbrook track athletes. Larry was a standout in track and field at Rye Neck HS and got a chance to interact or compete with many White Plains folks during his time.

During our brief interview, Larry pointed out that the first person he met from Winbrook was Lawrence Mosley around the time he was in the 8th grade. He remembers when they used to have field day track events at Highlands Middle School, and he met Mosley during one of those events. They became friends from that time on and stayed in touch over the years. Larry knew pretty much all the White Plains track athletes but became good friends with them when he attended college at Florida A&M University with Otis Hill, Charlie Sasser, Charlie Saunders, and Butch Mabry. Larry also knew Ronald Moss from Winbrook well who later married one of his classmates from Rye Neck High School named Debbie Doughty.

Carl Reed stands out in Larry's memory as one of the greatest 220-yard runners to ever come out of White Plains. He remembers when the White Plains High School relay team set the National High School "880 relay" record and Carl was on that team. Larry tells the story of the time he ran into Carl later in life as an adult on the streets of White Plains and shared with him how proud everyone was of his accomplishments and how impressed he was of him as an athlete. At that stage of Carl's life, it seemed as if he had moved on from those days and didn't care much to bring them back up...as we all knew "Carl was Carl" ...very quiet and never cared much to be the focus of attention, but it was good to have a brother like him from Winbrook in the mix. He made a tremendous contribution to the legacy of White Plains track and field and we are forever grateful. Rest in peace.

Larry also remembered Joe's brother, Sensei Mack from White Plains, who opened one of his first karate schools in Mamaroneck above the Elks Club, during his earlier years of teaching the martial arts around Westchester County. Additionally, Larry was a member of a local band led by Jimmie Robinson called "The Jive Times" who played the college circuit and occasionally opened up for the Societies from White Plains, one of the hottest bands in the region during that era. Larry was also friends with George Anderson who was the drummer for the Societies and with the Cain brothers, Bill and Kenny, from 11 Fisher Ave in Winbrook. He visited HL Greens on Main St. and the Carver Center on Lexington Ave., thereby, making him an "Honorary" member of the White Plains crew!

CHAPTER 19

SPORTS ACHIEVEMENTS AND STORIES OF SUCCESS

By Joe Mack

The following are some of the people from Winbrook and the White Plains Region who reached the highest level of achievement in their sports careers. We do not claim this to be a complete listing of all who reached that pinnacle of achievement and it is only intended to provide a sampling of those we were able to uncover:

Mal Graham - Was the first person from Winbrook to make it to the NBA when he signed with the Boston Celtics. He later became a federal district judge in Massachusetts after retiring from the NBA.

Larry James - Was a standout track star at Villanova University who went on to compete in the 1968 Olympic Games in Mexico City, Mexico winning a gold medal in the Mile Relay and a silver medal in the 400 Meters in world records times. Larry also joined with teammates Otis Hill, Carl Reed, and David Jackson to set National Relay records in high school and the Penn Relays, as well, with the team being inducted into the Hall of Fame for both institutions.

Art Monk - Played professional football for the Washington Redskins his entire career and eventually became the first person from Winbrook inducted into the Football Hall of Fame in Canton, Ohio.

Dennis Morgan - A professional football player who signed with the Dallas Cowboys after college and had a sensational career, at one point holding the record for the longest kickoff return In Cowboy history!

Channing Frye - An NBA player who was born in White Plains and played for the New York Knicks for part of his career.

Sam Bowers - Played professional football for the Chicago Bears.

Jim Gray - Played professional football for the New York Jets and the Philadelphia Eagles.

Grover William Jones Jr. - Played professional baseball for the Chicago White Sox.

Bill Cain - Played professional basketball for the Portland Trailblazers.

George "Duffie" Rooks, Sr. - Played professional football for the Green Bay Packers, Baltimore Colts, and several other teams, he later became a police officer in White Plains and went on to become the first Black Captain of the police force. His son, George Rooks, Jr., also became a professional football player, and his daughter, Yvette Rooks, is inducted into the White Plains High School Hall of Fame.

Nate Collins - Played professional football for the Chicago Bears and the Jacksonville Jaguars.

Ricky Edwards - Played professional football for the Chicago Blitz.

Harry Jefferson - Was head coach for the high school basketball team and played professional football for the New York Giants.

Herschel Jacobs - Became the New York State Boxing Champion in the Light Heavyweight Division when he defeated Hal "TNT" Carroll at the Westchester County Center.

Renaldo Snipes - Fought for the World Heavyweight Championship against Larry Holmes and lost by TKO in the 11th round.

Carl "The Truth" Williams - Fought twice for the World Heavyweight Championship. Once against Larry Holmes and once against Mike Tyson, losing both fights. He later defeated Bert Cooper for the USBA Heavyweight Championship and defended his title nine times before losing it to former world champion Tim Witherspoon.

Grandmaster Dr. Shihan William Mack - achieved the highest martial arts rank obtainable when promoted to 10th Degree Black Belt in the Universal Goju Kai System of Karate by Great Grandmaster Arron Banks and was inducted into the World Oriental Martial Arts Hall of Fame at Madison Square Garden in New York City.

Grandmaster Tony Watts - Mastered the art of Wing Chung Kung Fu and achieved international fame and recognition for his teachings and displaying the mastery of skills in his schools throughout New York City.

CHAPTER 20

MILITARY FRIENDS FROM WINBROOK AND OTHER PLACES

By Joe Mack

In addition to folks from Winbrook who served honorably in the military services like Cliff Livingston, Charlie Saunders, Eric Rhodes, Willie Hodge, Ricky Holdip, Gamal Mack, and Joe Mack, there were so many others not mentioned due to loss of contact or memory recall over the years but each of them also deserves the honor respect of their place during this time as well. Including Greenburgh residents like Billy Sudderth III, George Marshall, and Louis Archer. Let it be known that everything reflected throughout this project is intended to represent all who served in our era and others who came before us to lead the way.

This points out the fact that White Plains, NY, and its "Winbrook" influences are known throughout the military community nationally and worldwide. Our story has been told often, as a result of the people from the neighborhood who served and shared their memories of home and community with their friends in uniform at various duty station assignments over the years.

Joe Mack, for example, had several close friends that will be mentioned here but this story is certainly not the complete picture. It is one, however, that could be told many times over by each of our military veterans.

As Joe reflects on the military connections during his career, he can recall close friends like:

Charlton "Big G" Gregg, Dallas/Ft. Worth, TX, US Navy, First Class Religious Program Specialist. Big G was one of Joe's roommates and closest friends in San

Diego and he heard all the stories about Winbrook and White Plains, NY in Westchester County. He also met Mom Mack; Joe's wife, Thelma; sons, Gamal and Tahir, and daughter Imani. Big G can tell you even today about Joe being stuck with some friends on the Tappan Zee Bridge one winter during a snowstorm!

Hiawatha Clemons, Houston, TX, US Navy, Chief Warrant Officer WO3 Boatswain's Mate. Joe and Clem were stationed together several times in Lakehurst, NJ, San Diego, CA, and Norfolk, VA. Clem traveled with Joe to White Plains on more than one occasion and met most of Joe's family in Winbrook during those trips. He was one of Joe's mentors in the Navy and may he rest in peace.

Billy "The Trumpet Man" Sudderth III, Greenburgh, NY, US Marine Corps, Corporal, Reserve Infantry Unit. Bill and Joe connected in Marine Corps Boot Camp when they realized they were both from the White Plains, NY region and have been the best of friends since that time. Bill is a world-class musician who went on to achieve legendary fame as a recording artist with Atlantic Starr's band after completion of his time in the service. Bill is known throughout the Winbrook and White Plains community as one of the best musicians to ever come out of the area and is respected to this day for his skills and high level of achievement.

Johnnie Rush, Mamaroneck, NY, US Army, SPEC 4 Artillery Unit. Johnnie and Joe grew up together both in Sumter and New York. Their families were close, and Johnnie hung out with Joe in White Plains frequently. Johnnie was a highly intelligent brother who could accomplish almost anything he put his mind to, and he and Joe were constantly trying to outdo each other, just like siblings in a family which only made them closer and better overall in their achievements. May a dear friend and my brother in the struggle rest in peace.

Art Moran, Richmond, KY, US Navy, Senior Chief Electronics Technician. Art, who was first stationed with Joe in Guantanamo Bay, Cuba, and later in San Diego, got to know White Plains as well as anyone. Art was a highly skilled bowler and also someone with a deep interest in martial arts, in addition to being a devoted family man. Art, no doubt, heard all the stories about Joe's brother,

Karate Grandmaster Shihan W. Mack, and his schools over the years.

Ken Foster, Richmond, VA, US Navy, Third Class PO, Radio Communications Specialist. Ken and Joe met in San Diego when Joe oversaw the base track and field team at Naval Training Center and Ken was a world-class track athlete at the time. They became close as teammates and competed together on the west coast in the process. Ken met Joe's brother, Sensei Mack, during his lone trip to California and they hung out for a few weeks and had some fun going to several Dojo's for training sessions as the Winbrook legend continued to grow.

John Eldridge, Chicago, IL, US Navy, Senior Chief Supply Specialist, John, and Joe were stationed together in Norfolk, VA and managed the local base basketball team along with several other endeavors. John got to know a lot about Winbrook through Joe over the many years they worked together and met many of his family members in the process like Vince Wilson, Mom Mack, and the Holiday Family from Columbia, SC.

Clarence Franklin, Youngstown, OH, US Navy, Senior Chief Radio Communications Specialist. Joe and Clarence both served as Instructors at the Navy's Fleet Training Center Command in Norfolk, VA, and often hung out together. Clarence can tell you all about White Plains, as well, and even traveled there with Joe to meet his mother in Winbrook and hang out with his brother in New York City for the weekend. Clarence no doubt remembers stories about this trip and his Winbrook experience until this day.

Pink L. Kennedy, South Oak Cliff, TX, US Navy, Chief Electronics Technician. Pink and Joe completed basic training in the Navy together and have been close friends since that day. They were both stationed at Treasure Island, CA near San Francisco where they completed specialized training in Navy Radar Support Systems. Pink also traveled to White Plains meeting many of Joe's family and friends at Winbrook and can tell a few stories of his own.

E.C. Shingles, Harlem, NY, US Marine Corps, Lance Corporal Infantry Specialist. EC is a martial arts expert and the closest in location to Joe's hometown, next to Billy Sudderth. They completed Marine Corps Boot Camp training together and traveled frequently to visit each other's families back and forth from White Plains to Harlem. In addition to hanging out at Winbrook, EC also got firsthand exposure to martial arts training in the Universal Goju Style of Karate at Joe's brother, Grandmaster Shihan Mack, school during his visits and will long remember his matches with Bahru Seward, Rasheen Reed, and several of the other students in the class.

John Holden, Pasadena CA, US Marine Corps, Lance Corporal Combat Infantry Specialist. Joe and John met during their tour in Vietnam and John took Joe under his wing to show him the ropes when he arrived. They were both good singers and would spend endless hours in the fox hole telling stories to each other about White Plains and Pasadena while harmonizing songs by the Temptations just to pass the time and get through the night. The two were "hardcore" Marines but would sing songs from time to time which brought a brief moment of relief and enjoyment to their troops during those difficult and trying times in the War.

While this is only a small sampling of the Winbrook military connection, imagine what would be like for all those who served to exchange stories of how their lives were influenced by the White Plains and Winbrook community. These stories were spread around the nation as they traveled and shared them with their friends at various duty stations, Air Force bases, Army Installations, on Naval Ships, Marine Corps Detachments, and the like.

"Semper Fi" Brother Holden, Brother Sudderth, and Brother Shingles. "Fair Winds and Following Seas" to all my Navy Ship Mates, Army and Air Force brothers as well, and may "Big Clem" and "Big John" rest in peace.

CHAPTER 21

CHANGING OF THE GUARD: MOVING FROM THE '70S TO THE '80S AND BEYOND

What We Know About the Generations that Followed

Gamal Mack Interview

Following are summarized excerpts of a live interview done with Gamal Mack from 159 So. Lexington Ave. The information presented will begin to set the stage for a transition in the Winbrook era from the 1960s and 1970s into the 1980s. Gamal is now a member of the Orange County Fire Department in Orlando, FL, and provides his perspective below:

By the mid to late '70s, most of the generation from the '60s had moved on. Many of them went off to colleges or trade schools. Several of them joined the military like Eric Rhodes, U. S. Air Force, Rickey Holdip, U. S. Marines, Cliff Livingston, U.S. Army, Charlie Saunders, U.S. Army, and ultimately Joe Mack, U.S. Marines, and U.S. Navy along with so many others not listed. Some entered the workforce and moved away and, sadly, a number of them passed on before us...

During this transition point, the landscape around White Plains was beginning to change with a lot of Black families moving out of the Winbrook Apartments and relocating to different parts of the city or just leaving the area altogether. There were, however, a number of the younger folks like Jason Rhodes, Gamal Mack, Mark Mabin, Geraldine Mack, and Kenny Mack Jr., Anika Coram, Jamorah "Kai" Mitchell, Charles (Chucky) Boston, Corey Kent (a baseball phenom...a great pitcher), Derrick Chatman, Xavar "Toby" Dotson,

Venal Ford, Marvin Green, Ben Williams along with a host of others, who still kept the essence of "Winbrook Pride" alive and served as a transition platform from that era of the '60s and '70s into the '80s and beyond.

Gamal remembered that during his era Lexington Ave was a two-way street and not a one-way like it is today. You had to cross the street to go to the Spanish store or the variety shop, with the dry cleaners right next to it and the barber shop around the corner. He recalled that back then people had to look both ways to cross the street and this was something children in the buildings learned to do early on. Gamal also remembered another business on the same side of the street as 159 called Esaw's and described it as a breakfast and lunch place, right next to the little Jamaican store that sold beef patties. He talked about continuing up Lexington Ave towards Post Road where there was a flower shop on the corner and being able to get a good corn muffin with a slice of butter from Esaw's in the mornings before going to school.

Gamal talked about growing up in building 159 on the 8th floor, apartment 8G, where he lived until joining the Navy like his father before him. He recalled friends in the building like Mark Mabin, 1st floor, Dacia Banks and Zotica Medina, 2nd floor, and Michelle Moore, 4th floor. I can't remember the people on the 5th and 6th floors too well, but I do remember the lady on the 7th floor named Vann and she had a son named Jeffrey who I hung out with every so often. Gamal also added, "On the 8th floor with me was the Rooke family, whole family of girls I never saw a boy in the house and if there was a boy in there, I felt sorry for him (laughter)."

Gamal indicated during his interview that the thing that sticks out in his mind was the Community Pride displayed by the people who lived in Winbrook. He remembers when his group would be taken up to Ferris Ave to play games like basketball and football against the other teams, they were no longer recognized by the buildings they lived in, like 135...159...11...33 or 225. It was then just Winbrook (The Projects), as they would be known playing whatever team showed up that day. He said they played the poor man's version of football, nerf ball, where they just got out on the field and basically tried to kill each other, didn't sound like rules were much of a factor. Gamal describes having that same pride when he went down to play at DeKalb Ave off Mamaroneck Ave and down to Lake St. as well, pointing out how it was funny that all of these apartment buildings around town, each had a different view as to who they were. At the same time, there was a common connection to the other buildings and sense of identity. He remembers how there would always be battles between 135 and 159 on the bus rides to and from school as to who was the best, "Awh man 135, you get off on the 2nd stop, it was all about 159."

Sadly, some of the memories people will also have is about the drug trade as it became more and more prominent...it was kind of headquartered in 159. Late '70s – '80s it went from people just selling like marijuana and then crack and crack exploded. I remember when the Slater Center was built across from Bethel Church, we were kinda...what was this place being built? Our cub scout meetings used to be down in the bottom of 11 Fisher Ave in those little community rooms. When Slater Center got built, we thought, what is this place?

The next thing you know we had our meetings in there, in this community type place and then you saw this explosion of drug traffic come in. I remember a video they showed and the dangers of someone getting involved with heroin use, fast forward to today and people are talking about the opioid epidemic. I remember seeing that in the '70s. What do you mean epidemic? This has been going on for a long time and there were good people in the community who were trying to steer us away from bad things back in the '70s.

Gamal reflected on several of his mentors at Slater Center during the time he grew up. First mentioning his Grandma, Mary Mack, who was in charge of his cub scout troop, as he recalled how people from all the five buildings showed up at first but then it kind of whittled down to a smaller number after a while. Through Mom Mack's determination and efforts, Slater Center ended up with a solid cub scout pack. Another name included was Chief Henry Williams who was in charge of the boy scouts and mentored the cub scouts in the center, as well. Also, of note was Bump Robinson who started a Drum Corp out of Slater Center. Gamal stated the people in the Corp were mostly from Winbrook and Ferris Ave. He said, "It wasn't much, we had drums and marched in a few parades, but it was one more way to get us involved and off the streets when we weren't playing football, basketball, baseball whatever."

When reflecting on the good times they had, Gamal thought of the many block parties in the playground. Noting that area was referred to as the big basketball court and the shade house. Saying "Not supposed to be in the shade house, something shady going on in the shade house." He remembered that the Bennetts would come out from time to time and set up their "DJ" equipment and people would come from all around, it was music, music, music.

Gamal recalls another fond memory: Now something that many people may not remember if it was in the summertime and you were thirsty, but you didn't want to leave the block party. You wanted something cool and refreshing but didn't want to go around the block to the Spanish store...Joey, the ice cream man would always pull up just when you needed a soda or ice cream or something. There were three white men who could come into the neighborhood and nobody would mess with them, the mailman because he was usually delivering something in an envelope that somebody wanted, Richard the fish man because he's selling fish and there was always a long line and Joey the ice cream man. Joey was the first person to ever give me credit, it was 5 cents or something like that. He passed away not too long ago, and he was known throughout White Plains, Greenburgh, and all around. Everybody looked on his Facebook page...we did love Joey.

Gamal also remembered looking out his 8th-floor window 8G and being able to see the playground clearly. His Grandma would say "Don't go where I can't see you," so since she could see 90 percent of the playground, that left him a lot of places he could go. He recalled that at times when the block party was for the older crowd, he could look down and still be a part of the party by just watching. He remembered speaker wire and extension cords being hung out the Bennett's windows to keep the partying going. When he thought of basketball games in the playground, Gamal said Adrian Bennett comes to mind. He recalled that Adrian was a great basketball player who could hold his own with whoever showed up, although playing on the courts at Winbrook was not necessarily a ticket to the NBA. Gamal was quick to point out that his own basketball game was decent but that he would leave the court when the other, more serious, people came on.

When reflecting on some other specific names that came to mind, Gamal thought of Kenny Mack Jr. who he went to school with. Pointing out that he had a sister named Geraldine Mack and they lived on the 6th floor in the same building, 159, where Gamal and his family lived on the 8th floor. I remember that because if I ever got a piece of mail & it was labeled G. Mack and there was not an apartment number on it many times we would pass each other and she would say I have your mail because back before apt numbers were on addresses you'd see G Mack no one would know which one and since I was so young no one would think that I get any mail, but since Grandma had me into acting doing commercials every so often a piece of mail may come in for me. Geraldine's son, Chucky, and his younger son Akeem were Kenny Mack's nephews so it was a family thing, families always stuck together. He was kind of a short guy and he always had a word for you and I never saw him disrespect anybody, I saw him get disrespected by people, but people like him were the ones you saw who later on in life you reflect back on and go "that's how you treat people."

Gamal continued his thoughts on the respect he saw paid to others in Winbrook.

The biggest thing is older people were respected at a level you don't see today. As much as people were selling drugs, they were like hey - move out the way let them through, now a young person coming through they wouldn't say anything but an older person coming through hey move out the way They may not always help the person, but they'd open the door -or say hey, move out the way someone's coming. Even the police who used to come in the neighborhood, now they knew what was going on, the guys in the neighborhood knew what was going on --but you could see some level of respect there -ok you don't see me do anything ok you're not going to toss me so those types of things you saw just a general sense of respect, that is earned and given to people --People from church, Calvary, Bethel they were given a level of respect--people who would never set foot in the church, they could die and not have a funeral in the church but they saw the deacons and the pastors come through it was their upbringing, these were people they were told to respect and they did.

Gamal went on to point out that his generation seems to be where things started to change in terms of having that level of respect as he moved into middle school and high school. That's when he noticed that when people were sitting on the stairs in his building, and they saw someone coming they would just move to the side instead of getting up and letting that person pass and then sitting back down.

Gamal also shared his thoughts on the buildings being phased out and what lessons he learned growing up in Winbrook.

Sadly, it is probably time, the buildings were not brand new when I lived there and after time, 30 years H.S. reunion coming up next year, and add 18 years that is almost 50 years that is a long time for a building to stand. You know Winbrook went through some renovations, added some things, paint jobs and at some point, the building does need to be replaced. I look at it and, what do you do with the people?

These are people if you look at White Plains where are they going to live? There is no place for affordable housing anywhere, not just White Plains. The nice thing about Winbrook is you did have a sense of community living in Winbrook, you grew up there, you could tell your kids you know, I went to school or I used to go to church with this person, I think you should talk to them. Bright side is that the building is going away and it's sad, but the memories remain.

You can talk to people about the numbers in Winbrook, just the numbers, don't have to say the street name and people can geographically know, boom, right here 33 in the middle, 11 on the street, 159 and 135 were right there, 225 on the back side, we didn't know north, south, whatever, that was the back side...and then it changed the name of Grove Street, used to be Grove Street, why is it now that one little section Dr. Martin Luther King Blvd? Does it always happen in every Black city somewhere? Dr. Martin Luther King Blvd has to be associated with a project area. You'll never find a predominantly white area, like where I live in Orlando, FL, with a "President Barack Obama Way" --good luck finding it.

Gamal provided further memories of his days in school and how some of the things have changed in White Plains since then:

Well, I'll compare it against a few other places I mentioned like Ferris

Ave, Dekalb, and Lake Street. We (Winbrook) were 5 buildings, nobody else had 5 buildings, we were the big kids on campus. We didn't all go to school together until 5th grade, then White Plains shifted elementary school from K-6 to K-4. We had 5th – 6th at Highlands, 7th and 8th at Eastview, and then High School 9th – 12th on North Street, main campus so we didn't really come together from all these different neighborhoods until 5th grade.

Some people went to George Washington, some went to Post Road, some went to Mamaroneck Ave school, and when we came together that's when people started asking who's from the projects. That's the bus going to the projects and we knew that was our badge of honor. That's our neighborhood. There is a Netflix special out called the "Get Down" - Nelson George is one of the primary producers-- and it chronicles the beginning of the hip hop era in the '70s and goes back to some things that I remember at Winbrook definitely-- the Blackout. Anybody who remembers the '70s will remember the Blackout, what they kind of portray in that special --I'm not going to give away too much- is how hip hop took really off during the Black communities because of the looting that took place --when the power went out at Winbrook we didn't have generators, we were in the dark and elevators were out.

We didn't have any emergency lighting in the stairwells, these are the things we had to overcome, and it was scary, but we overcame those things, and we grew. In the film "Get Down," for anyone who has been to the health department in White Plains, well that building is in the show. You'll have a shock when you watch it --I know that building! They pay homage in the show to a lot of different areas in NYC and for me, that was a White Plains thing, not a Winbrook thing but you couldn't walk from the Winbrook projects to Mamaroneck Ave. and say I've never been to the health department because all of us went in there to get a shot, we didn't have managed health care, many of us were going there for medical needs.

Things around town we got into--the courthouse was open--wow look at that big building over there…we remember nothing about that building except the Scarsdale diet doctor, when he was killed the trial was held there. That was a big trial of the century and it got our attention because it was right across the street from Winbrook. Those are some of the things you remember and later on in life looking back at things, I realize I had a great upbringing in Winbrook, friends, family, enemies that kind of shaped things for me living in some of the places I've lived like San Diego, DC area, and now Orlando.

You look at some of these places that are impoverished. I look at some of those impoverished areas and realize where you live, doesn't determine where you are going to go. You have an opportunity to make the best of the situation. If you are going to stay here, stay here and do something to better the community.

Gamal's closings comment centered on the sense of loss when the Winbrook Projects are gone:

The biggest sense of loss is history. Winbrook's history is unwritten -- Winbrook's history right now is untold. Hopefully, this book will be a project that can be like a time capsule as new people move into this area and see these new buildings that are being built. The new buildings look nice and hopefully, they will stay that way but the thing that will be lost is the history. People won't remember things like the laundromat in the basement of 33, wow, that was a place where we hung out from time to time. 11 Fisher having the rec rooms in the bottom, I bet right now someone couldn't tell you there were rec centers in the basement of 11 Fisher Ave. Voting used to go on in there and I remember going to Bethel Baptist Church because that was the next precinct to vote in.

Living in Florida with the voting thing we had a few years ago, people who have moved here from NY say, oh why can't they vote here like they vote in NY? All talk about the same thing, you walk in, pull the curtain, pull the lever. I was very fortunate watching that growing up. I think what could be missed when those buildings come in is that the community won't have those things and they won't be able to translate that into remembering their past to build upon their future.

There's definitely a bright future for the Winbrook area and that bright future is in the people who lived there. Whether they are 1st generation 2nd, 3rd generation or immigrant from another country or another part of the city, there's a bright future for them if they just know a little about the past of that place.

There's blood in the past, there's gold in the past, but in the future is really where I hope that something good comes out of it.

AZ3 G. Mack

Joe Mack's eldest son - Gamal Mack - Winbrook - A Navy Man! Around 1990

CHAPTER 22

HISTORICAL PERSPECTIVES

By Joe Mack

White Plains, NY and the Winbrook Projects: A Historical Perspective.

While writing this book, Jamal Koram and I made a number of trips to White Plains and talked to a number of folks along the way. In many of these conversations, historical facts related to the Projects and White Plains were brought up that we thought were not only appropriate to be included in this work but necessary.

In our conversations with Charlie Morgan, Cliff Livingston, Wilbur Rooke, Brother Surya Peterson, Artie Bennett, and several others; along with our review of the book pictorial "On The Streets Where We Lived" by Harold A. Esannason, we discovered that Brookfield St., which intersected Fisher Ave and is no longer there, was at one time a "haven" for a number of Black-owned businesses in the years before Winbrook was developed and shortly thereafter. Prior to urban renewal, Brookfield Street and several other areas around the city were home to businesses such as:

- Lee's Funeral Home
- William H. Sudderth Insurance Company
- McAdam's Brothers Barber Shop
- Ideal Shoe Repair Shop
- Crescent Barber Shop
- Perry's Funeral Home
- Johnson's Shoe Repair
- All State and NY Day Taxi
- Gibson Appliance
- Thomas Demolition

- Esaw's Luncheonette
- Evie's Beauty Salon
- Brookfield St. Dry Cleaners
- Brookfield St. Lumber Yard
- Butcher Shop (Brookfield Street)

There was also a Black-owned Hotel on Lexington Ave where the police station now sits.

Pastor Gillette, the minister from Mt. Hope Baptist Church, opened the first credit union for Blacks in the city.

Other memories and notes of historical significance we discovered included:

- 33 Fisher Ave. was the first building to be built in the Winbrook Project development.

- Finding out that 159 So. Lexington Ave was the only building that had four bedrooms.

- Buddy Simmons had the first Black-owned gas station in White Plains on the corner of Lake St. and Kensico Ave.

- Rosa Kittrell was the lady who started the Carver Center and now has a park dedicated to her name on Fisher Ave.

- Joseph Davis was the first Black fireman hired in the City of White Plains.

- Martin Rogers was the first Black police officer hired in the City of White Plains.

- Mom Mary Mack, 159 S0. Lexington Ave. Apt 8G, Posthumously, received an official "Proclamation of Service" from the Mayor's Office in the City of White Plains.

- Madeline Jenkins and Chief Henry Williams have a Memorial Playground placed in their honor at the front of building 159 So. Lexington Ave.

- Among the first families to move into Winbrook were the Miles, the Lynks, and the Simmons families.

- The Livingston Family moved into Winbrook from Brookfield Street in 1958.

- The following families all came to Winbrook around the same time: The Rooke Family, The Pines, the Grandersons, the Walkers, the Rhodes, and the Martins.

- Winbrook was initially state-funded but became federally funded in 1982.

And more...so much more.

This represents only some of the historical highlights from our meetings and interviews collected over the past five years or so, however, it by no means covers the complete historical picture of the Winbrook or White Plains story. The reader is likely to find a more complete historical depiction of the Black community in the days before development of the Winbrook community in a pictorial book entitled "On The Streets Where We Lived" by Harold A. Esannason, which gives a thorough account of life for Blacks living in White Plains in the early 1900s, with many supporting pictures from that era. It provides an insightful and historical perspective of life and times in the White Plains community and the beginning of Winbrook families during the turn of the century and beyond.

Baba Jamal Koram "The StoryMan" taking in a lesson on Chess and Life from Dr. Grandmaster Shihan W. Mack following his interview - Ferris Ave Dojo, White Plains, NY

Photo 2019

CHAPTER 23

RACIAL INEQUALITY TODAY AND WHERE DO WE GO FROM HERE? HOW WE AS A PEOPLE CAN MOVE FORWARD IN TODAY'S SOCIETY

By Joe Mack

If someone were to canvas the five buildings today, they would find quite a different environment than the one that existed in the late '60s and early '70s. Most of the Black families from that era have been relocated or have moved on to different communities around the city or to other states. While there are still a few families living in Winbrook that we knew growing up, they are now the "exception" rather than the rule. The buildings are culturally diverse in that there are a significant number of Hispanics, some Blacks, and even a few white families living in the remaining apartments. This is in contrast to Winbrook being a predominantly Black neighborhood in the past. The one common theme, however, is that poverty remains a factor in the lives of the residents. Let's reflect for a moment on how living in a low-income environment impacts the lives of its inhabitants. There is a loss of the sense of safety and security because everyone is just trying to survive and going after the same available resources in the community. Folks are more inclined to create schemes or develop other means to get an edge in the "fight" for survival. As in all parts of the country, whenever there is an increased amount of tension or higher levels of stress evident in our society, these conditions are amplified threefold in communities like Winbrook. Black folks now and have always been in a struggle for racial equality and have found it increasingly difficult to achieve these goals despite efforts put forth by various social programs over the years. There always seems to be an equal and opposite force designed to hinder any real progress and to keep the "caste system" mentality firmly in place. So how do we, as a culture, move forward and obtain a measure of success in a society where all must find a way to co-exist in a peaceful manner? There have been many proposals regarding this question, and they all have a measure of merit. Subsequently, there is no one correct way or foolproof method to solve this nationwide dilemma. There are, however, several concepts that can certainly be a recipe for success towards achieving this goal.

- First add in a few pounds of compassion and concern for others, this includes cleaning up rather than tearing down our communities, being supportive of those with programs for youth in our neighborhoods, and offering a helping hand, when needed, through volunteer programs and the like.

- Next sprinkle in a portion of increased interest in education, especially at the lower grade levels. A solid foundation makes for a well-built and longer-lasting house. This should include a return to classes like Civics so that our students grow up understanding how our government is supposed to work, knowing their rights in society and how to properly address them when issues develop.

- Add a slightly tossed helping of knowledge regarding our elected local officials. Find out who is running for office and what their record has been in the past on issues related to your community. How they've voted on certain issues in the past is a matter of public record. Research it, know it and if you don't like it...vote them out.

- Bake in a success model of Energy, Effort, Faith, and Grace. Let it simmer and serve when ready.

While these are only some of the ingredients to add to the pot in an attempt to reverse inequality in communities like Winbrook, there is so much more to be added. Think of ways to reach out and connect with others to create a unified effort towards this cause.

CHAPTER 24

FUTURE PERCEPTIONS

In this section, Joe Mack and Baba Jamal contemplated several ideas to help bring back the spirit of the Winbrook community each year for those of us still around and our descendants. The thought was to put a few things in place that would encourage us all to reach out to others we know of in various locations around the country and to lay the groundwork for an annual get-together in one of these locations. Some of these ideas include but are not limited to the following:

Future Perceptions - Ideas for Future Gatherings

- Recovery of "Winbrook Pride." Reconnect with each other, rekindle and recover. How to engage in future White Plains activities and setting up activities in other cities as well. "Getting in Stride with Winbrook Pride!"

- Organize and establish a phone tree, zoom, or other contact media to begin making plans for our annual get-togethers at various locations.

- Reach out to find out who would volunteer to be the point of contact in each location and establish the locations we desire to target for trips, in addition to White Plains.

- Establish a centralized point person for collection of contact data, etc. so that we can communicate effectively with each other as needed.

- Gather ideas from others as to how we'd like to go about planning, collecting information, and communicating with each other during the early stages of this process.

We hope that while reading this book you were able to think about and record for future reference several of the following key points:

1. What lessons were learned and what were your thoughts as you reflected on the memories recorded?

2. Capturing these memories
   - what is its value?
   - why is it valuable to you or others?

3. What characteristic traits did you develop out of your Winbrook experience that stayed with you throughout life?

CHAPTER 25

FOUNDATIONS FOR COMMUNITY DEVELOPMENT

While contemplating thoughts on what we could leave for future generations and communities like our own, Joe Mack presented his ideas for Community Service Training - July 13, 2016, White Plains, NY, Winbrook Workshop, at the Stamford Marriott, Stamford, CT.

This is designed to provide ideas that could put in place a training system that would provide a blueprint for developing a positive and forward-thinking path for well learned and productive members of the community from youth through young adulthood.

What we would want to see accomplished in our "new" and old communities.

Create a working model from below.

Community Involvement - Five Preliminary Stages of Development and Training from Youth to Young Adult

Consider experiential learning

Throughout the course of this process, there is evaluation/measurements/ feedback and recognition by allowing them (the students) to present what they have done and how, to an informal group of program elders.

1. **Learning Phase/Apprentice**

   Needs to be a learning foundation. Students here are gullible - will need to be taught beneficial and correct principles. This is a curious phase of life and at this stage, they are susceptible to false teachings. There needs to be an apprenticeship capacity/stage that ensures students avoid following the wrong lessons or paths in life.

2. **Progressive Phase investigating/questioning/molding ideas into personal learning areas to teach**

   Young Folks are developing ideas and investigating new areas of learning; questioning given information and new interests. They are molding the learning to fit what they are capable of and what they can do/how they can do it/what ways it can be brought to focus or to use...

3. **Perfecting Phase/testing, refining ideas to Master an area of learning to be used to benefit the community: this is the phase where expertise is applied to the needs of the community.**

   Mature Young Adults: Perfecting/testing/refining/mastering what areas of learning they have chosen for themselves to measure if it is doable and what they can master and be able to teach or put into action.

4. **Supportive Phase: Oversee/guiding/reinforcing what they have learned to apply**

   In this phase folks will have roles to guide and oversee what they have been providing and learning, in a supervisory capacity, making sure that the needs as identified are being met and the proper personnel and resources are made available and applied to these needs.

5. **Wisdom Phase:**

   In this phase seniors are providing insight and wisdom on community needs, to apply correction, direction, and stability. This is primarily a group of seniors serving in a supportive capacity, to be called upon as needed to balance and correct inconsistencies among the working staff or among the volunteers. Also, to provide direction in these situations serving as mentors, counselors, references, and providing guidance to correct any unstable situations among community activities. Also, this group offers insight into the services, financing, supervision, advocacy, and development of projects/programs/and long-term stability within the community.

CHAPTER 26

IN MEMORIAM

IN MEMORY OF - This chapter reflects the names and, in some cases, comments about people we knew and can recall who are no longer with us except in spirit and memory. They were mostly from Winbrook but several others from the region will be recognized as well, some with brief annotations. Paying honor and respect to the memories:

These are reflections of sisters and brothers from around and in the Winbrook area of White Plains, NY in the '60s and '70s who have since passed away, but whose memories are with us, and will not fade. In no way is this intended to be a complete list but as one elder friend put it, "My babies deserved to be cherished, the good and the not so good." They need to remain with us; in our minds, hearts and souls; as testimony to and for our sacrifices, our resilience in an age of warfare as it was for our fathers and mothers before us, to a changing of lifestyles, and a dissolution of communities. Brazen challenges to our creativity and resilience. So long as they are remembered, and their personalities and stories are told, their legacy will live on among us. These pages are our contribution to them remembering two decades when we sacrificed for our loved ones and created a time of enjoyment in their lives.

We pay tribute and honor to the names of our friends and family listed herein knowing that there are more...so many more…Amen.

Reaching for the Soul - Remembering the Winbrook Spirit ...Remembering Our Brothers and Sisters Who Passed This Way

In honoring those that have gone on before us Baba Jamal and Joe Mack reflected on the names, they have been made aware of during their interviews. Please excuse any omissions or errors in listings during this section:

Several Names Stand Out that Everybody Knew:

Otis Hill - one of the greatest athletes to come out of the area and a person of class and character.

Larry James - The Mighty Burner. Larry was a world champion in more ways than one. Well respected and loved by those who knew him.

Carl Reed - Carl was the quiet storm on the track. Nobody could touch him in his favorite event, the 200 meters.

Dennis Morgan - Dennis was the epitome of hard work which ultimately landed him as a star in the National Football League.

Rasheen Reed - a karate master who grew up under the training of his teacher and mentor, Sensei W. Mack.

Jerome "Bump" Robinson - Another Legend in the city of White Plains. Bump represents Ferris Avenue and was instrumental in improvements and youth programs throughout the city. He was active in the Community Action Program (CAP) and also a viable member of the Thomas H. Slater Center on Fisher Avenue. Bump was also the founder of The Thomas H. Slater Drum Corps in the mid- 1980s.

Our Hearts Also Reach Out to The Memory and Spirit of The Many Others Listed Here:

Baba Jamal Remembers:

Bennie Bennett - A cool brother who was well known throughout Winbrook. A fun-loving ladies' man and he could handle the rock on the courts. Respected by all the brothers in the hallway (159) for his status among them. He and I maintained mutual respect as well. He was picked up one summer night from in front of 159, on a minor charge, and we never saw him alive again. Different stories were told, but I guess none of us will ever know what actually happened that night when the police got him downtown. Bennie was tall, slim, and dark-skinned. Folks always thought he was Coon and them's brother. Another "young un" trying to negotiate his way through the world, going through the thickness and wilderness of South Lexington.

Jerome "Bump" Robinson – A legend in the city of White Plains. His name became synonymous with anything happening in the city. He was one of those brothers that stayed home when others left for college, jobs, etc. and he rose to high levels in everything from politics to local activities around Winbrook. I remember him singing on the street corners and I would occasionally join in for a note or two. This laid the foundation for groups like the Societies, the Sensations, and the New Band, who later rose to stardom and became Atlantic Starr.

John Lee – Ballplayer extraordinary! He played WPHS basketball, and I considered him a quiet storm on the courts. During a basketball tournament at the Westchester County Center, I don't remember who we were playing, but it was a final's game. The ball was passed in from behind the opponent's basket. Time was closing in fast, and we were behind by a point. The opposing team had lined their defense up under their basket, with seconds to go. Davy Jackson had enough room to inbound, so he whipped the ball into John Lee, and then he took off down court. Now Davy was an all-star track man. John Lee got the ball, and immediately the opposing team surrounded him and thought they had him, but he whipped the ball around himself, dribbled in front of the opponents, lifted the dribble, and threw a half-court, two-handed BOUNCE pass to Davy Jackson, who scooped it up on the run, left the ground and dunked for the winning points, at the buzzer. Talk to us! WOW!

Eric Rhodes - Eric was a killer on the courts! One of the best basketball players to come out of Winbrook. Eric also had a good sense of humor and kept something going on with the fellas to brighten the day. Eric played on the high school basketball team but was also a member of the JABO Rims and New York Poles during the summer league games played around the community.

Willie Foster - He was a man for all seasons. A highly intelligent brother who was aware of everything going on in the projects. We were close and I respected the way he carried himself. I remember when they tore down an old store up on Ferris Ave and put up a basketball court. One day Willie stood on the court and dunked the ball backwards from a standstill! That was the first time I had seen something like that. We talked about a list like this the last time I saw him in

White Plains, little did I know at the time he would be on it.

Ronald Moss - Ronnie was always quiet and a good scholar. He was considered one of the leaders among the guys and was close to his family. Ronnie was good in every sport and a standout in basketball, track, and football...he played them all at the high school. We miss his quiet strength and leadership.

Eugene Battle - Eugene was my little foster brother and we lived together in Greenburgh. We hung out together all the time, especially around the time when I got hit by a car on Tarrytown Road and nearly died at about 12 or 13 years of age. When I came out of the hospital months later my foster family had moved to White Plains and carried Eugene with him. I was placed with another family and didn't see him as much after that.

Raymond Jordan - The last time I saw "Frog" was one afternoon, of all places, we were on a side street in Harlem, NYC. We hadn't seen each other in years, but we recognized each other right away. We gave strong greetings. I asked if everything was cool. He assured me he was alright and was in his right mind. "I know what it looks like, but I'm O.K. Loon." It's easy to weep when you care. God Bless My Friend Raymond "Frog" Jordan and rest his soul.

Freeman Beville - a laid-back brother who could handle the rock on the basketball courts. Few had a smooth rhythm and amazing moves when he was on the court. He was a quiet brother with a tremendous basketball game who could play any position on the court. Didn't talk much but didn't have to, his game did that for him.

Joe Remembers:

Adrian Bennett – The youngest of the Bennett brothers and the one most laid back, until he got on the basketball court. Adrian was only about 4 '11' 'but was as quick as lighting and would make passes you couldn't imagine, reminded me of Earl "The Pearl" Monroe. We always joked around and he kind of looked up to me because I was a bit older. I loved being on the court with him as a teammate. I last saw Adrian at Grasslands Hospital after the car accident he was in on the Bronx River Parkway. It was the same time my brother was there following the shooting incident and I stopped by Adrian's room. He couldn't talk but he was alert, and he knew I was there.

Bennie Bennett- The oldest Bennett brother - we didn't converse too much, except to say hello. He always seemed to be doing something important, even when he was just walking through the hallways, but I'll leave that one alone.

Rickey Holdip – "Don't lose your head, you need your head…your brains are in it!" This was the quote Ricky left in the high school album the year we graduated. We were close during that time and he talked to me about how cool it was. We hung out together a lot and did a lot of things together, including catching the Mamaroneck Avenue bus to go caddying at Ridgeway Park golf course. Ricky had an ok game on the courts but was better known for his smooth walk and the rap game he tried to run on the ladies. We kind of lost contact when I left for the Marine Corps, but I saw him one day when I came home in uniform and he said, "Man I want to try that." We joked for a while and I later found out that he had gone into the Marines, but it didn't work out for him long term.

Larry Hodge – He was my younger cousin from South Carolina who ventured up to White Plains for a time. Larry was a debonair and well-mannered, ladies' man who drew a lot of attention for his good looks and laid-back approach. He later joined the Army and would make frequent trips back to Sumter to see family members. It was on one of these trips that he got engaged in a fight in the role of peacemaker, and instead, ended up becoming the victim. My heart will always go out to Larry. As his big cousin, I often tried to give him encouragement and advice to which he took to heart, and I believed he had a bright future ahead of him.

Tommy Hodge - Another of my cousins from South Carolina who moved up to White Plains and lived with his sister, Bae "Sharon" Mitchell, and brother-in-law, George Mitchell down on Lake St. for a while. Tommie "Snake Eye" was well-liked by everyone he met, and he also trained at the Universal Goju School of Self Defense with my brother, Sensei Mack, so he knew how to take care of himself. Tommie often hung out in Winbrook where he came to check on my mother, Mom Mack, but also spent a significant amount of his time in 33 Fisher Ave. apartments where he most likely had several close friends and acquaintances. I miss Tommy even today; he had a way of uplifting the spirit of those around him and could sing like a gospel hummingbird...runs in the family.

Freddie Mack – Freddie was Kenny Mack's brother. He was always respectful and could be found most of the time in the hallway at 159. Freddie was looked up to by the younger brothers coming in and out of the building and we never failed to greet each other in our travels. He ended up having problems with his kidneys before the age of 30, and health-wise, things went downhill from there. Yes, Freddie Mack was a pretty decent ballplayer too.

Bae Mitchell - Bae was one of my close cousins as well who, much like my mother Mom Mack, came to White Plains from Sumter, SC, and made it her home. Bae lived in Winbrook and on Ferris Ave. before settling in the Lake St. apartments where she spent the remainder of her life. Bae was also a martial arts expert in the Universal Goju School and a dedicated member of Calvary Baptist Church. Bae married George Mitchell and raised her daughter, Jamorah Kai Mitchell, and the rest of her children in the Winbrook Community. Rest in peace my cousin, you are sorely missed.

Reggie Roberts – A smooth little brother about 5'6." He and his sister Nancy were the heart and soul of 33 Fisher Avenue. We talked often because I also lived in 33 Fisher at the time, and he always seemed upbeat. In fact, I saw him earlier in the day before that night at H. L. Greens, where we used to party on the weekends. R.I.P. my brother.

John Lee - The last time we talked was in front of 159. John Lee was an alright brother. The last time I saw him, I was crossing Lexington Avenue in front of 159 and he was coming from the Spanish store. He looked so different, I hardly recognized him - so small and frail. But we made eye contact and greeted each other, we talked for a minute and I asked, "Man, how are you making it?" He replied, "Not too good Mack, I got caught up with this illness and can't shake it." I wished him well and told him I would pray for his recovery. It was the last time I had a chance to talk with John Lee before I got the word a few weeks later that he was gone.

Johnnie Rush – "Big Johnnie" was my cousin and "Brother from Another Mother." Johnnie and I last talked when I went down to Sumter for my Aunt

Lila Mae's funeral. He was having some health issues at the time, but we were still able to bring back some memories of old which brought a smile to his face before we parted. I told him to take good care of himself and avoid anything bad for his health, not realizing that would be the last time we would see each other. Rest in Peace Big John, your legacy will live on in your family and those of us that knew you best.

Larry Rooke – Larry lived in Winbrook, down the hall from me in 159. I saw him almost every day. A kindhearted brother who always seemed to get along with everyone. I never saw him in a fight or even an argument. Larry was an excellent artist and would draw pictures that everybody wanted to get. He didn't come out much but when he did, he got everyone's respect. JM

George Williams – George was my predecessor at Westchester Community College as President of the Afro-American Society. When he graduated to go to a school in the mid-west, he pulled me aside and gave me some encouragement about becoming the President of the Afro-American Society and facing the challenges ahead. He said he would keep in touch and always be available for advice. I last saw him driving away in the Volkswagen that he cared a lot about. I thought about that car when I heard about the car accident he was involved in at school…

George White – Not everyone knew George White, because he was from Greenburg, and didn't venture too often into White Plains unless he was with one of us. I got to know him well because he ran track, and also had a good heart. He would hang out on some weekends with me and our friend Alden Mitchell "Splouse," (Jamal's childhood friend too) George would hang out with me and Alden, and joke about everything we could imagine. He was truly dedicated to running and enjoyed it.

Glenda Coleman - Glenda was small in stature but big in "Heart". She lived up the hill off Lexington Ave and was well-liked by all. Glenda seemed to be serious about everything she did and always had a kind word for those she knew. I last saw Glenda shortly after coming home from the war. She was on her lunch break from work, and we greeted each other, I wished her well.

Kenny Cain - Kenny was Bill Cain's younger brother and he held up the family tradition on the basketball courts as well. Kenny and I hung out and played a lot of basketball together, especially on the playgrounds and as members of the JABO Rims. Kenny thought he could do a little bit of everything: dance, sing, box but basketball was what brought him fame.

Bonnie Gilchrist - Even though Bonnie was born in Elmsford, NY, she made White Plains her home and that is where she left her legacy. My last encounter with Bonnie was at my mother's funeral when she came to share her condolences. Bonnie worked as a nurse's aide in White Plains Hospital and cared for my mother many times in her later years and for that, I will always be grateful.

Garry Livingston - Garry was Cliff's younger brother and we saw each other pretty much every time we came in and out of the building 159. Garry was a tall brother, about 6' 5" in stature, and was always quiet and peaceful, didn't say much but was always aware of everything going on in the five buildings. Remember Garry with a smile.

Kenny Mack, SR. - Kenny was the Man! Boxer extraordinaire, he could hurt you with the left hook... but he had a heart of gold. Kenny was my mentor in the boxing gym and, because we had the same last name and both our families lived in 159, many people thought we were related. I miss my brother and last saw him playing his stand-up acoustic bass guitar on the porch in front of 159. He said, "Hey Mack, listen to this" and he played one of the songs I taught him when he first got his instrument. I said, "Man you got it!" ...that touched my heart.

Shirley Archer - My sister-in-law from Greenburgh. She married my brother, Shihan Mack, and I got to know her as a kind-hearted and loving relative. Shirley had a pleasant personality, a wonderful smile, and a heart to help others. I last saw Shirley at June's funeral and she still had that enlightening smile.

June Sudderth - Bill's sister from Greenburg who everybody loved! June was refreshing and pleasant to be around. She was admired by all and set the perfect example for the young ladies growing up in her neighborhood as to how they should carry themselves. June was like a sister to me, and our conversations were always encouraging and uplifting.

Eric Rhodes - Eric lived in the next building from me 135, and we got to know each other well. He was another of the dynamic B-Ball players from the area and played on a team I helped put together called the JABO Rims, he couldn't be stopped on the court and made a lot of people pay the price for trying. Eric was a fun-loving person who didn't mind getting in a joke or a laugh on the fellas whenever he could.

Cleo Daniels - Big Cleo was one of my boxing teammates in the Cage. He was a heavyweight who could hit like a ton of bricks. I was young and Cleo had already turned professional. He would often pull me over and give me some pointers about the fight game. I always remember him telling me, "This fight game is a hard hustle Mack, make sure you train hard but get your education cause that's what will carry you."

Herschel Jacobs - Jake was another of my boxing teammates at the Cage. He was a big man (light Heavy) with a kind heart. Jake taught me a lot as well and he probably put White Plains on the Boxing map with his sensational skills which enabled him to win the New York State Championship. I'll always remember him coming down to me in the locker room the night I got hurt in a boxing show in Montrose, NY, and telling me how impressive I was in the ring that night before the injury happened. He said I would have to decide for myself if I wanted to stay in the fight game, but then he showed me all the scar tissue he had around his eyes and said this is the price you may have to pay so make sure that's what you're willing to do. I appreciate your compassionate encouragement and miss you Big Brother.

Kathy Reed - Kathy was the younger sister of Ben, Jr., and Carl. The older sister to Rasheen (Jimmie), Brian, Debbie, Patty, and Penny. She was a key part of the Winbrook community growing up. She knew someone in just about all the buildings and offered the kind of friendship cherished by those who knew her. Just like the rest of us, Kathy played in the circle and the playground growing up. She was also at the show mobiles cheering on the likes of the Sensations and the Societies while harmonizing songs with them such as … "What's Your Name..."

Carl "The Truth" Williams - I pay tribute to Carl Williams because of his legacy and what he left behind. Carl was among the best boxers to come out of White

Plains during the Cage era and left a lasting impression for others to follow. He was a slick and fast, hard-hitting heavyweight who could hold his own with anybody in the ring, including world champions like Larry Holmes and Mike Tyson. Carl ran up a string of impressive victories over his career and gave everybody in the White Plains community a renewed sense of pride.

Marvin Lewis - Marvin was a big brother with a gentle heart. He was well respected throughout the community and was involved in activities to help bring more programs for the youth in our neighborhood. Marvin also played basketball for the JABO Rims during the summers in the early '70s and was a dominant center whenever he was on the court no matter who he was matched up against.

Cedric Thomas – Cedric was a member of the White Plains High School record-setting track and field relay teams of the '60s. He was well respected throughout the Winbrook community and always greeted you with a smile. Cedric was smart, sincere and a tremendous athlete who will always be remembered.

Winbrook sadly had what many remember as the first fatality of the Vietnam War. **Glenn Andre Sheppard**, Marine Lance Corporal, 3rd Marine Division, 3rd Battalion, 4th Marines, I Company, grew up in 135, was an only son who never should have been drafted. His mother sought assistance from the Red Cross, and he was scheduled to return home one day after he was killed in Vietnam. His name is inscribed on the Vietnam Veteran's Memorial in Washington, DC (Panel 16e, Line 28.)

Other Names to Be Honored During This Section Include but Are Not Limited To:

Carolyn Hazelwood, Patricia Horton, Ralph Jamison, Albert Lewis, Patricia Ogburn, Walter Sutton, Louise Taylor, Barbara Lynk, Eugene Battle, Leon Higgs, Glen Smithson, Raymond Mitchell, Ozzie Mitchell, Joyce Cain, Hammy Randolph, Frank Pine, George Andrews, Foster Turner, Winston Roberts, George "Mooney" Randolph, Bobby Archer, Michael Rhodes, Herb Moss, and Ronald Moss.

And More…So Many More…

Winbrook

By Baba Jamal

Just a patch of where you're at

Knowing that

It took longer to demolish

Our beloved bricks

Than to build a

Neighborhood where friendships stick

Find a story, and pass it on before you lose it

Keep a story and pass it on, but don't abuse it

It's Truth…fades fast like that

Pass it on, for who is here and for who is coming

And for those who are gone

Most of them, too soon

Pass it ON!

Find the land and neighborhood

Recall the past in every generation

Adding lines to times that won't follow if

We won't speak …Tell the stories of coming and going and being

Remember. Find the land and the neighborhoods

Recall the past

Let it be what it is. Understand that Winbrook is more than Brick
It's family ties, it's still I rise
It's Spirit and Prayer
Deposited everywhere
Here and there, North, East, South, West
May our memories, joys, sadness, and
Our challenges, our families, and our friends
Reunite in Spirit here and whenever we can:
Winbrook Pride
White Plains, NY

CHAPTER 27

FINAL THOUGHTS

OUR LAST TRIP

By Baba Jamal

In the late Spring of 2020, Joe and I traveled up to White Plains, in what we believed would be our last visit before publication of the book. It wasn't, due to the COVID 19 pandemic, so we set sites on a later time. We figured that publication would be complete in time for the annual summer gathering, a part of summer events at Winbrook, which were well attended from neighboring townships, and a "homecoming" for many, who grew up in and around Winbrook....it didn't happen. Not this year. Not at the "Kensico Dam," or elsewhere. This "Pandemic" showed up and TOLD us what was going to happen to the project (no pun Intended) or The Projects!

Before we left Winbrook 135 So. Lexington Avenue was being demolished, crumbling before our eyes, and we left town with a couple of 135 Lexington Avenue "bricks." I imagine that my brick may have come from the 7th floor.

We decided that we would continue to put the final touches on the book, and maybe even extend it, but to have it complete by summer's end, 2020. To our dismay, the pandemic extended throughout the rest of that year and continues to this day. Damn.

Ending of an Era - Lasting Memories:

By Joe Mack

One of the final trips I made to Whites Plains and Winbrook, as we knew it, was to bury my mother, Mom Mack, from 159 South Lexington Ave. I was living in Richmond, VA at the time and working as a high school counselor. I would hang out from time to time with my cousin, Vince Wilson, also from Sumter, joking around and playing basketball whenever we could. Vince was a great basketball player, who played on both the collegiate and semi-pro level, but he couldn't handle my "no look" passes and finger roll!

The news of my mother's passing hit hard for me and when I told Vince about it, he said "Hey man, I know you'll need to go up early and I'll drive up there with you." I'll never forget the amount of comfort and support Vince provided during that time, not only on the trip up but all the way through the entire process of the funeral. I'm forever grateful to my young cousin and feel blessed to have someone like him in my life.

Mom Mack was stalwart and a pillar of the Winbrook community, a neighborhood legend in her own way. She worked constantly with her church - Calvary Baptist, and Chief Henry Williams, and others to build up the Winbrook cub scout and boy scout programs that were run out of the Slater Center. She was also a lifelong volunteer with the Red Cross.

Up until her health began to fail in her later years, Mom Mack served as the eyes and ears for other parents in the buildings, as well, whenever their sons and daughters were outside playing. Mom Mack treated them all like they were her own and didn't mind correcting them if they got out of order, it didn't matter who they were. I can remember a number of times she'd chased the pastor's sons off the streets in front of the buildings if things didn't look right and made them go home. Rev. Phifer later thanked her for doing so and let his sons know, "when Sister Mack speaks, you'd better listen." That's just the kind of person she was.

My heart will forever be burdened with the loss of a parent who taught me how to live, love, and respect others even if we don't always agree. She ran a strong single-parent household and made sure my brother Shihan, my sister Lil, my son Gamal, and

I had the spiritual foundation we would need in life to get us through the many challenges that would come our way. I find peace in knowing that our mother lives on in us each day.

As Baba Jamal and I come to the close of this project we want to take time to thank each of you who have had the opportunity to read these stories and share our reflections. We hope you have enjoyed taking this journey with us as much as we enjoyed writing it. If you come away with anything, let it be that our days in White Plains and the Winbrook community were not in vain. We have attempted to be as honest and as accurate as we could be in capturing the events of our era, while also being mindful of any memories that may be too painful to bear and remaining respectful of that as well. We understand that some names or specific events may have been missed, which couldn't be helped but hope that the essence of the Winbrook experience can be found in some way for all.

Finally, while there were certainly trying times living and growing up in an area that was not always treated kindly in terms of the support and resources needed to sustain a viable livelihood, as this book reflects, much greatness came out of our community and from those five buildings as well. As Valerie Simmons told us during her interview for this project, there were glorious and wonderful days growing in Winbrook as a child and she ended by stating

"It wasn't all bad...no, it wasn't all bad."

May peace and blessings be with each of you as we continue our journey into the next phase of our lives.

May we always remember that...what we do today matters and it's what we leave behind for others that live on forever.

Front view of 159 S. Lexington Ave. The hub of Winbrook during the '60s and '70s

Photo 2018

BIBLIOGRAPHY

Dodson, D. W. (1969). *High school racial confrontation: A study of the White Plains, New York, student boycott* [Pamphlet]. White Plains Board of Education.

Esannason, H. A. (2011). *On the streets where we lived: A pictorial study of African Americans living in White Plains, New York from the beginning of the twentieth century.* Published by Harold A. Esannason.

White Plains High School, NY. (1968). *Oracle 68* [Yearbook]. White Plains High School Library.

White Plains High School, NY. (1969). *Oracle 69 W.P.H.S.* [Yearbook]. White Plains High School Library.

Newspaper Articles:

Haggins, B. (1933). The Pathfinders Club Offers Recreation, Service, Dignity. *The Daily Press* (White Plains, NY).

1st Winbrook Tenants Move in Next Week. (1950, June 22). *The Reporter Dispatch.* (White Plains, NY).

First 24 Families to Move Into Winbrook in Next 6 Days. (1950, July 25). *The Reporter Dispatch.* (White Plains, NY).

BIOGRAPHY

Joe Mack's Biography:

Joe Mack was born in Sumter, SC, and moved with his family to White Plains, NY during his teenage years where he graduated from White Plains High School in 1968. Joe attended Westchester Community College in Valhalla, NY where he served as President of the Afro-American Society and was the first black student to play on the football team at that college. Joe received his bachelor's degree in social sciences from the State University of New York at Albany and his master's degree in counseling and community services from Norfolk State University, Norfolk, VA. He served in the US Marine Corps during the Vietnam War era before completing a 22-year career in the US Navy as an Electronics Specialist and educational services counselor where he obtained the rating of Master Chief Electronics Technician, the highest enlisted rate that can be obtained while in service. Joe Mack also coached and competed on Navy track and field teams at various duty stations during his career and later coached several members of the "All Navy" track and field program who were part of the Navy team that won the Military Intra-Service Track and Field Championships in the 1980s. After completion of his Navy career, Joe Mack served as a therapist working with troubled youth in a residential treatment program in Virginia before going on to become part of a team conducting a major national research study on identifying and preventing juvenile delinquent behaviors at the University of Virginia in Charlottesville, VA where he was the Senior Research Assistant Coordinator. Joe then transitioned to the Henrico County Public School System and worked at J. R. Tucker High School where he served as a school counselor and head coach of the school's track and field team.

Joe is an accomplished martial artist and boxer who has also competed as a Masters Track and Field athlete for a number of years, winning several championships during his era. He presently works with the Virginia Association of USA Track and Field in addition to being a founding member and head coach of the Pony Express Masters Track and Field team in Richmond, VA.

Joe Mack currently resides with his wife, Thelma, in Chester, VA and serves as an independent consultant for the 180 Degree Support Services in Richmond, VA co-owned by his youngest son, Tahir Mack, and business partner, Douglas Hood.

Baba Jamal's Biography

Baba Jamal was born James L. Coram in Grasslands Hospital, a few short miles from Greenburgh, NY, the ancestral home of his father's generation. His great-grandmother, and great-grandfather, and their children moved to Greenburgh from Virginia. He grew up in the communities of Greenburgh and White Plains, NY, and graduated from White Plains High School in 1968. Baba Jamal obtained his bachelor's degree from the State University of New York at New Paltz, his master's degree from State University of New York at Albany, and an educational specialist degree from the University of Virginia, Charlottesville, VA. In time he went on to become known as "Baba Jamal Koram, The StoryMan", one of the greatest African American storytellers of modern times. Baba Jamal served as past president of the National Association of Black Storytellers and has performed at festivals, colleges, and universities as well as many libraries, schools, and social events around the country bringing an Afro-Centric approach to his art that distinguishes him among contemporary storytellers. He is an accomplished author, educational consultant, producer, and recording artist who has appeared on numerous national television and public radio shows. Baba Jamal currently resides with his family in Virginia.

Made in the USA
Middletown, DE
05 November 2023

41807005R00146